In the Blast Zone

Catastrophe and Renewal on Mount St. Helens

About the Spring Creek Project:
The challenge of the Spring Creek Project for Ideas, Nature, and the Written Word is to bring together the practical wisdom of the environmental sciences, the clarity of philosophical analysis, and the creative, expressive power of the written word to find new ways to understand and re-image our relation to the natural world. For more information: http://springcreek.oregonstate.edu/

About Long-Term Ecological Reflections:
In a program that will continue for two hundred years, writers visit sites at the H.J. Andrews Experimental Forest and other charismatic landscapes, such as Mount St. Helens, to create an ongoing record of their reflections on the relation of people, forests, and landscapes changing together over time. For more information: http://www.fsl.orst.edu/lter/research/related/writers.cfm?topnav=167

In the Blast Zone

Catastrophe and Renewal on Mount St. Helens

edited by Charles Goodrich, Kathleen Dean Moore, Frederick J. Swanson

original line drawings by Ann Zwinger

Oregon State University Press
Corvallis

The paper in this book meets the guidelines for permanence and durability of the Committee on Production Guidelines for Book Longevity of the Council on Library Resources and the minimum requirements of the American National Standard for Permanence of Paper for Printed Library Materials Z39.48-1984.

Library of Congress Cataloging-in-Publication Data
In the blast zone : catastrophe and renewal on Mount St. Helens / edited by Charles Goodrich, Kathleen Dean Moore, Frederick J. Swanson.
   p. cm.
 Includes bibliographical references.
 ISBN-13: 978-0-87071-198-5 (alk. paper)
 1. St. Helens, Mount (Wash.)—Eruption, 1980—Environmental aspects. 2. Ecological succession—Washington (State)—St. Helens, Mount. 3. Plants—Effect of volcanic eruptions on—Washington (State)—St. Helens, Mount. I. Goodrich, Charles. II. Moore, Kathleen Dean. III. Swanson, Frederick J. (Frederick John), 1943-
 QH105.W2I58 2008
 979.7'84043--dc22

                    2007040282

Oregon State University Press
121 The Valley Library
Corvallis OR 97331-3411
541-737-3166 • fax 541-737-3170
www.osupress.oregonstate.edu

Contents

Foreword by Scott Slovic   vii

Introduction   ix

Maps   xviii

PART I

Coming Back to the Lady, *Ursula K. LeGuin*   2

Change, Survival, and Revival: Lessons from Mount St. Helens,
   Charlie Crisafulli   10

The Way to Windy Ridge, *Tim McNulty*   17

PART II

In Endless Song, *Kathleen Dean Moore*   22

Volcanic Blues; or, How the Butterfly Tamed the Volcano,
   Robert Michael Pyle   28

Mount St. Helens, *John Calderazzo*   36

On the Ridge, *Robin Kimmerer*   41

In the Zone: Notes from Camp, *Tony Vogt*   47

To Mount St. Helens, *John Daniel*   52

PART III

A Gardener Goes to the Volcano, *Charles Goodrich*   56

Evolutionary Impacts of a Blasted Landscape,
   Jerry F. Franklin   62

Mountains and Mosses, *Nalini M. Nadkarni*   70

Everlasting Wilderness, *Christine Colasurdo*   77

Science Tribes on Mount St. Helens, *James Sedell*   84

PART IV

Two Stones, *Scott Russell Sanders* 92

Nature's Shaking Keeps Me Steady, *Susan Zwinger and Ann Zwinger* 99

What if I Chose? *Kim Stafford* 104

Languages of Volcanic Landscapes, *Frederick J. Swanson* 105

PART V

Pearly Everlasting, *Gary Snyder* 114

For Further Reading 117

Contributors 118

By Way of Thanks 123

Foreword

"Mount St. Helens," in my boyhood imagination, was one of the "big mountains up in Washington State," a place—like Rainier and Adams and the peaks of the North Cascades—for serious climbers, for adventures of the body. In 1980, after I had left Oregon to attend college, St. Helens blew its top and made itself known across the nation. I was living in Philadelphia that spring and when my father came from Eugene to visit a few days following the eruption he mentioned that he'd observed ash floating some 30,000 feet in the air all the way to the East Coast.

I haven't been thinking much about Mount St. Helens during the past two decades, as I've moved from state to state, continent to continent. But it became clear to me, when I had the opportunity to read the manuscript of *In the Blast Zone: Catastrophe and Renewal on Mount St. Helens*, that many people *have* been researching and contemplating this special place for a very long time, since well before the eruption that made St. Helens a household name. What was once a place, at least as I understood it, for climbers and adventurers, has become a place for thinkers and dreamers, a source of ideas.

This collection of poetry and essays emerges from a July 2005 camping trip and educational event at Mount St. Helens, orchestrated by Oregon State University's Spring Creek Project for Ideas, Nature, and the Written Word, that brought together many of the leading writers and ecologists of the American West, including newcomers to St. Helens and some who had been studying or informally observing "the Lady" for many decades. The resulting collection is a thorough and authoritative narrative of the mountain's famous eruption in 1980 and its ecological renewal over the course of two and a half decades. But many of the pieces collected here go well beyond the specificities of Mount St. Helens' story, exploring on a more fundamental and universal level the phenomenon of environmental change, guiding readers to think carefully about how we use such words as "catastrophe," "disturbance," "loss," and "recovery." One comes away from reading this manuscript with a powerfully transformed view of Mount St. Helens and volcanoes in general, carrying in one's imagination ideas of green moss and blue butterflies, birdsong and wind, ideas that have now begun to complicate the image of St. Helens as a stark post-eruption moonscape.

As an anthology, much of which is lyrical rather than analytical, this is not a scholarly volume exactly. And yet the more *literary* contributions to the book are impressively rigorous in their vivid descriptions and emotional truths, while the somewhat more analytical essays are authoritative and engaging in their consideration of topics such as "biological legacies" and the types of language used in describing and explaining landscape. Many of the writings here bear a clear, oft-repeated message: that the story of Mount St. Helens is one of change and *renewal*, despite the scale of the volcanic blast that captured the public imagination in 1980. In essence, then, this is an extremely hopeful work, one that suggests the fundamental durability of nature. The ideas about natural processes and the meaning of nature in human experience expressed in this collection are powerful and accessible enough to be of interest to a wide range of readers, from scientists to humanists, to the general public. As a scholar of environmental *literature*, I find this to be a rich, multi-voiced symposium, surprising in its diverse textures of language and its consistent focus on the theme of renewal. I read it myself with delight and fascination, taking particular pleasure in its elegant interdisciplinarity—its inclusion of statements from novelists, ecologists, poets, natural historians, philosophers, and geologists. The collection is organized in a way that highlights the diversity of voices and themes.

The 2005 gathering at St. Helens marked the twenty-fifth anniversary of the momentous eruption and launched this book project. While only a handful of people were fortunate enough to participate in that gathering, the rest of us can contemplate the lessons of Mount St. Helens and savor the vibrant voices of those who were there by way of this book, which I hope will find its way into the hands of scholars and artists in all of the disciplines represented by the contributors (and then some), citizens of the Pacific Northwest, folks who had bits of volcanic ash from St. Helens land in their hair and on their cars back in '80, volcano freaks everywhere, and anyone who's fascinated with and concerned about patterns of catastrophe and renewal in nature and culture.

Scott Slovic, University of Nevada, Reno
Editor, *ISLE*

Introduction

Landscapes tell stories, if we know how to listen. When Mount St. Helens erupted on May 18, 1980, the story most people heard seemed to be almost entirely about violence, danger, and devastation. But even as rescue efforts continued for the people missing on the mountain, scientists went up to the volcano looking for other stories. They wanted to see how the landscape would respond to these enormous disturbances, and they brought along some reasonable hypotheses. But much of what they saw and learned was so radically different from what they expected that their new findings have significantly changed several branches of ecology.

Writers and thinkers have a long history of regarding the mountain, as well. Since the eruption, they've been gauging the volcano's effects on the regional culture, wondering how these changes in the landscape will affect people's lives and imaginations.

What would happen, the editors of this volume asked, if we invited a group of scientists, writers, and other interesting people to go up to the mountain, to camp together for a few days, to share their particular kinds of knowledge, their informed perspectives on how the mountain had changed and how it had changed us? And what if we asked them each to write something that drew on both their expertise and their personal experiences, to consider what those changes might mean for how people live their lives? Would this help us to hear more kinds of stories about what it means to live in a volcanic landscape, in a world of constant change?

With those questions in mind, we proposed to host the Mount St. Helens Foray. We invited several forest ecologists, a couple of poets, a lepidopterist, a journalist, and a bryologist (a scientist who studies lichens and mosses); a singer/songwriter, a sociologist, a photographer, a stream ecologist, several writers of nature essays, and a writer of speculative fiction; also, a research ecologist who has spent most of his career—twenty-five years—doing field work almost exclusively at Mount St. Helens. (Biographical sketches of all the contributors may be found at the back of this volume.) We camped together on the mountain for four days in the summer of 2005, hiking, observing, reflecting, learning the ecology, sharing stories, insights, and ideas about the meanings of catastrophe, and about sources of renewal. This book brings together essays and poems by many of those who participated in the Foray, and several pieces by other long-time Mount St. Helens watchers. Together, they suggest a few of the many promising ways of approaching the question: What can the radically altered landscapes of Mount St. Helens tell us about how to understand nature and how to live our lives?

The Eruption

For two months in the spring of 1980, magma shoved up under the north flank of Mount St. Helens. On a Sunday morning in May, a huge landslide broke loose the north side of the mountain and slid twelve miles down the Toutle River valley, burying more than twenty square miles under rock, mud, and broken forest. As the mountaintop collapsed, it uncorked a super-heated groundwater system that had built up within the volcano. A steam-driven blast shot out to the north, ripping away the forests closest to the vent. Farther away, the blast snapped off trees, toppling them in patterns that mapped the direction of the force. The heat seared forests as many as seventeen miles from the mountain, leaving a fringe of scorched trees, the standing dead.

Searing hot pyroclastic flows spewed from the crater mouth and built up at the northern foot of the volcano, leaving a broad, barren pumice plain. Massive mudflows raced down rivers that drained the volcano, some traveling seventy-five miles to the Columbia River. A cloud of tephra, gray volcanic ash, boiled into the atmosphere and rode the wind to the northeast. Ash darkened the day and rained from the sky over a vast area of eastern Washington and beyond.

The diverse volcanic processes utterly transformed Mount St. Helens' forests, meadows, lakes, and streams into a complex mosaic of new environments. Closest to the explosion, entirely new landscapes replaced the old: a volcanic crater over a mile wide, where once a summit had stood; new lakes, ponds, and streams on the debris avalanche and at its edges; and square miles of seemingly sterile new land surfaces. Farther from the volcano, as much as three feet of fragmented mountain top blanketed the killed forest and beds of lakes and streams. Even beyond the blast zone, cool tephra snowed onto the land, collecting on branches, blanketing the moss, lichens, and foliage.

Geological processes continue to compete to shape the new volcanic landscape. Intrusion of magma into the volcano led to its collapse, but ongoing magma flows soon began building new domes at the rate of several dump truck-loads of rock a minute. The giant landslide drowned entire rivers, but new rivers began to carve watercourses across the pumice plain. The landslide blocked tributary streams, forming new lakes and ponds, which filled and drained as rivers cut new outlets.

Mount St. Helens exhibits strong, startling tensions also between geological and ecological forces. Geological forces, such as the deposition of tephra and debris, may have buried an area and destroyed its plant and animal communities. But as these deposits are eroded, new landscapes may be created where plants and animals begin to thrive, whereupon ecological forces become more prominent. In some instances erosion prevents plant growth; in other cases plant growth suppresses erosion.

At first, ecologists were stunned by what looked like a gray, lifeless landscape. Their initial assumptions were that this "moonscape" would only very gradually recover and that species would colonize the disturbed landscapes from the edges inward. But these assumptions were soon disproved. On research missions to the volcano within days of the eruption, ecologists were astonished to find surviving plants and animals emerging from refuges in soil, rotten logs, snow banks, and ice-covered ponds. These biological legacies of the pre-eruption ecosystems profoundly affected the post-eruption landscape. Now, twenty-five years after the eruption, the volcanic landscape is a patchy pattern of what ecologists call "hotspots"—habitats favorable for plant community development—and "coldspots"—places of persistent erosion where no plants or animals have established a home. Different ecosystems have responded at dramatically different rates: lakes and steep meadows have adjusted rapidly, but centuries will elapse before old-growth forests shade the slopes again.

The Mount St. Helens landscape now also maps human responses to the volcanic eruption. The conflicts over forest land management that had bedeviled the region for decades emerged again on this new ground. In 1982, two years after the eruption, Congress passed the National Volcanic Monument Act to establish an 110,000-acre Monument where "geological forces and ecological succession

[can] continue substantially unimpeded." Outside the boundaries of the Monument, private industries and the Forest Service rapidly "salvage logged" the toppled and standing-dead forest and planted conifer seedlings. The boundary between the Monument and private land is sharp and clearly visible across the hillsides. Planted forests develop dense tree crops quickly, creating productive but simple monocultures, visible as a thick hatch of trees. Mount St. Helens Monument's unplanted hillslopes bloom with a wild profusion of tree, shrub, and herb species and a corresponding diversity of insects, amphibians, mammals, and birds.

What Does It Mean?

What is the meaning of the volcano-blasted mountain? When blue lupines colonize a pumice barrens, what might be learned about catastrophic change and the chance for renewal? What do we know that we didn't know before about being human in a volcanic landscape?

First came fear. Ash and stones falling from the sky. Sizzling rock pouring down riverbeds. Ponds boiling into clouds. Stones floating like ice on water. "A mountain not acting the way a mountain should," the writer and volcano-watcher John Calderazzo said. The sound: like the end of the world. But also the shiver, the thrill in this power, the blast that everyone who was paying attention knew was coming. Then, from his observation point a few miles north of the mountain, geologist David Johnston shouted into his radio, "Vancouver. Vancouver, this is it!" as the pent-up volcano let go.

Then came grief. There had been people on the mountain. Fifty-seven of them died, all with names and hopes and secrets. So did elk and deer, fish and birds, marmots and bears. Untold thousands of animals were killed. And the explosion was a loss for people who loved the mountain itself, people whose families gathered there year after year, rested in the shade of giant cedars, launched canoes that rippled the perfect reflection of the beautifully symmetrical peak. What would they make of the loss of the peace of this place? And what would comfort them, as they mourned the cedar groves blasted into ash, and Spirit Lake, a sacred place turned into something more like a pulpmill lagoon?

And twenty-five years later, exhilaration and hope. "There is such singing in the morning," the novelist Ursula Le Guin has written of the Mount St. Helens landscape today. And it's true. If you wake early on the mountain, you will hear white-crowned sparrows and frog choruses and maybe even a meadowlark. They will be flitting around a grove of fir saplings, or fussing in willows at the edge of a marsh where beavers have dammed a backwater pond. Lupine spread purple over pumice plains, where there are deer and elk and black bear. Children walk the trails to the lakes, lifting puffs of ash, releasing the sweetness of fir needles under their feet.

It's hard even to know how to speak of this extraordinary transformation.

Is the volcanic explosion, as scientists would say, a "disturbance agent" that results in "change" and elicits an "ecological response"? What is gained and what is lost in the thinness of this language? The question is no sooner asked than the scientific language flowers into something like poetry—blast zone / singed zone / standing dead / ashed forest. Ash and tephra / nuée ardente, the glowing avalanche / pyroclastic flows—that precise, that true. And the poets turn their attention to the ways our lives are, in Robert Michael Pyle's words, "bent, changed, refracted, buffed, and scraped—in every way worked by the mountain." The philosophical issues are inescapable: What can the mountain tell us about the meaning of sudden and catastrophic loss? What can we learn from the mountain about what it means to heal?

When Le Guin came up to the mountain, sixteen months after it erupted, she saw "devastation on an enormous scale. One had to think of Hiroshima," she said, "but this was not human-made ... How to understand it?" What is the relation between human-caused and natural cataclysm? Standing in ash on the ridge just beyond the mountain's "ground zero," what might we learn of remorse and moral resolve? What can we learn—by way of contrast or comparison— about the losses in our own lives, the ground shifting under our feet, the uncertainty, the sudden disappearances of people we love, the dreams turned to ash? If we could understand a mountain as change through time, how differently might we understand grief?

And are these lupine-graced meadows a "geography of hope"? No sooner had the ash cooled than small, soft creatures began to emerge from their hiding places—frogs and chipmunks and salamanders. Seedlings that were sheltered by snow grew up to scatter seeds of their own. Entirely new lakes, ridges, landslides bloomed. Is this survival or recovery or creation—and what do these processes tell us about the sources of renewal in our own lives?

The mountain speaks of resilience—the toughness of life, the fragility of lives. It speaks of permanence and transience, of what endures and what passes away. It speaks of the beauty and insistence of natural processes that, given time, bring the mountain back to life.

The mountain stuns and humbles us with powers beyond human control, often beyond human imagining—a seven-mile-high chimney of shattered rock reaching from deep in the earth into the blue Washington sky. When the earth shrugs, we know in our spines that we are not the center of the universe, and certainly not the directors of its destiny. What do we make of this kick in the pants, this blow to the ego? This creative destruction?

Notes from the Foray

THURSDAY, JULY 21 — IN CAMP: We have cautioned everyone in e-mails that our camp will not be beside a babbling stream in a deep, forested glade, but rather on a bulldozed turnout where the gravel road forks, high on the windy, sun-scorched, volcano-blasted ridge between Bean and Clearwater creeks. There are no developed campgrounds this high up, this near the volcano. We have room for the caterer's kitchen trailer, a couple of 10- x 20-foot canopies for shelter from the weather, two port-a-pots, and not much more. We've worried that people will find the place ugly and forbidding, a scar on the Earth. But the pumiceous ground is covered with purple lupine, the weather, after a scorching afternoon, is cooling down nicely, and the view of Mt. Adams to the east is stunning. Everyone has brought their own camping gear and as they arrive they wander off to find places level enough to pitch their tents among the young alders.

Just as the sun begins to set, we gather for introductions on a hummocky human-made hill where hundreds of truck-loads of pumice were hauled and dumped after the eruption. From up here we have a full-on view of Mount St. Helens, the crater and flanks etched by deep shadows in the long evening light. Thin scarves of orange cloud stitch together the highest ridges. The mountain seems vibrant, imposing, and very close. As we settle into our camp chairs, a plume of ash and vapor erupts from the crater. We are well within the 1980 blast zone. Are we in any danger?

The mountain is covered with sensing devices. The seismic forecast calls for continued dome-building and minor steam eruptions, nothing more. But we are keyed up now, resolved to pay attention, to ask good questions.

FRIDAY JULY 22 — AT META LAKE: Blustery winds and rattling rain through the night. This morning, lightning over Loowit. Then more cold, blowing rain.

Crowding into the narrow dining canopy, we eat pancakes with our gloves on, tell each other about our relationship to Mount St. Helens, to volcanoes, to nature. Then we pile into the vans and head out.

Our plan is to hike from Donnybrook to Windy Ridge, a mile-long trail overlooking Spirit Lake that would bring us into close-up view of the crater. But the mountain is hidden in heavy clouds, the wind ferocious. Huddling together at roadside, we listen to Fred Swanson's thumbnail geological history of the mountain—catastrophic eruptions and summit re-building time after time over many millennia. But it's too cold and windy for hiking; we retreat to Meta Lake.

Tucked in amidst young, green fir and hemlock, a lakeside pier and a paved terrace. We sit on the stone wall in a big circle and dig into sack lunches, gradually warming up. When Ursula Le Guin was here in 1981, the summer following the eruption, she found unworldly devastation. Now she can't believe how green it all is. Ecologist Charlie Crisafulli, who has spent twenty-five years doing field studies on Mount St. Helens, tells us that the western toad, though declining throughout its range, is abundant here. And other surprises: many bird species—horned larks, rock wrens, savannah sparrows, western meadowlarks—that did not use the mountain habitat when it was deep forest have migrated into the area. Elk routinely trample his rodent-sampling traps.

The sun comes out, to audible sighs. We hike in to Ghost Lake, where everyone basks on the pumice beach, except songwriter Libby Roderick, who rolls up her jeans and wades into the water, singing. In the year 2000, the poet Gary Snyder came here with Fred Swanson. In his book *Danger on Peaks*, he wrote about touring the disturbance gradient from the blast zone outward, in a poem which ends—

> Out to Ghost Lake through white snags,
> threading down tree deadfalls, no trail work lately here

> ... I worked around this lake in '49
> both green then

Evening campfire on the ridge. Nighthawks dart amongst us, chasing the moths that mingle with sparks from the fire. Stories, poems, jokes. Full moon rising. Coyotes howling. Libby sings a new song she's been working on, "We All Live in the Big Volcano."

BIG steam plume from the mountain.

SATURDAY, JULY 23 — EVENING, BACK IN CAMP: Changed. Everyone seems changed.

This morning we decided we would make our hike from Donnybrook to Windy Ridge in silence. Already saturated with new ideas and insights, we were more than ready for some quiet reflection. We started hiking through green firs and arching elderberry shrubs, past shady grottos bursting with wild flowers. But soon we came out onto a barren, sun-dazzled slope where the trail clung unconvincingly to the crumbling mountainside. Spirit Lake rippled below in a mild breeze, much of its surface still clotted with dead trees.

Round the campfire this evening, we were shocked to hear how wildly different were our reactions to the day's experiences. While some of us had been exhilarated by the silent hike on the high exposed trail, others were cast down by the sight of a million dead trees afloat on Spirit Lake, scared almost witless by the narrow trail carved so precipitously into the crumbling slope. Along with our astonishment at the rejuvenation of the landscape, we all seem to feel an abiding desolation.

SUNDAY, JULY 24: Breaking camp. Rolling up tents, bagging garbage, packing the vans. One final group photo on the ridge with the volcano behind us.

After these four extraordinary days camped in full view of the caldera, what does the mountain ask of us now? Maybe just this:

to continue coming together, with science, song, and poetry—with the most careful thought, loving observation, and exact words—to imagine how we ought to live in a volcanic land. What does this mountain tell us about our obligations to all the wounded landscapes around the globe? What understanding might we carry away like vital seeds to sow in our own forever-changing communities?

"Birds have the gift of song," Robin Kimmerer reminds us. "And with the gift comes the responsibility to sing."

"In time, I will be an elder," adds Kim Stafford. "People will turn to me for answers, and I will turn to the mountain."

Charles Goodrich, Kathleen Dean Moore,
Frederick J. Swanson

Snowy volcanic peaks of the Cascade Range, stretching from
Canada to northern California, form the backbone of North
America. In the midst of this range, Mount St. Helens has
distinguished itself as the most dynamic, erupting far more
frequently than any other Cascades volcano during the past several
millennia. The 1980 eruption was notable for the wide range of
volcanic processes and their profound impacts on forests, lakes,
and streams. The collapse of the north face of the mountain and
the ensuing massive debris avalanche, mudflows and pyroclastic
flows, along with a blast that toppled the immense forest and left a
fringe of standing dead trees—these upheavals collectively affected
more than one hundred square miles. Along with the subsequent
responses of the land and the biota, Mount St. Helens has also
catalyzed new ecological, sociological, and imaginative thinking
about change, renewal, and the relationship of humans and the
land.

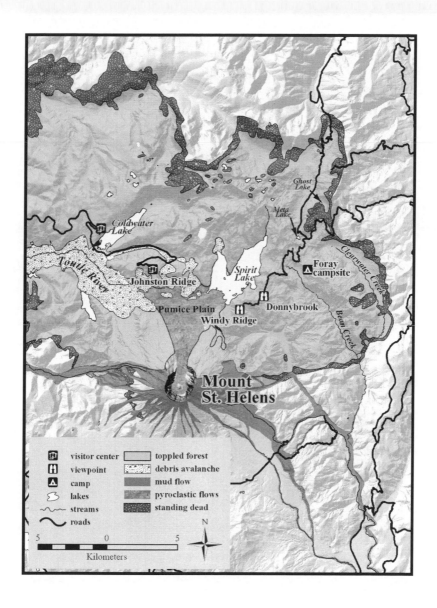

Part I

Coming Back to the Lady

Ursula K. Le Guin

Mount St. Helens has been my neighbor for more than forty-five years. If I look straight north out the window at the head of our bed, she is the first thing I see in the morning, dark in the dawn twilight, or floating pale above the mist at sunrise. My study windows look north too, and when the "mountain is out," as Portlanders say, I look up at her from my work again and again all day. Living in the shadow of the West Hills we don't see the sun setting, but we see the light of sunset on the volcano, subtle glories never twice the same.

When "the Lady" started shaking and doing strange things in 1979, my love of her beautiful presence became a driving interest, almost a fixation. While she was dormant I had made sketches trying to catch the pure line of her almost-but-not-quite symmetrical flanks and the clouds that wreathed around her head like veils. As activity increased and ash eruptions began to blacken the cone, I drew what I saw as best I could, sitting at my study window, using binoculars to bring details close. Experimenting then with chalk pastels, I found them a good medium for the drama of ash and cloud and snow going on there, sixty miles away overland and nine thousand feet up in the air.

The great eruption of May 18, 1980, was inaudible as well as invisible in Portland: the sound wave, in its majestic vastness, simply stepped over us, to step down in Eugene. There were clouds between us and the mountain. We heard about the eruption on the morning news. Not till late in the morning did the cloud cover break to let us see the incredible column of dust and ash rising thousands of feet (though it seemed almost immobile) over a blur of haze where the mountain had been. I watched it all day long. It never occurred to me till evening to turn on the television.

I missed many spectacular views of the eruption from news helicopters; but the real thing was there out my own window, the biggest thing I ever saw or ever hope to see.

I drew endless pictures that summer of the ashfall, the mountain's new, ragged profile, and the lesser but magnificent eruptions of the following months.

Reading an article about people who thought they'd foreseen the eruption in dreams, or who dreamed constantly about it, I recognized something similar to my own semi-obsession. Thinking it might be something I could write about, I put out an ad asking people to send me any St. Helens dreams they'd had before or after the eruption. Most of what came was not very interesting, but there was one marvelous letter: a young woman wrote she'd dreamed she was up on the west side of the mountain with a tree-planting group, the morning of May 18, and made a hair-raising escape on dirt roads in terror and growing darkness. An awful nightmare! But it wasn't a dream. She had really been there, and really did barely escape. For her to tell it as a dream was a perfect device. There was no way I could improve on it, and I only wish she'd found a publisher for it herself.

My friend the painter Henk Pander had been painting St. Helens' secondary eruptions all the year after the big blast, and he knew the photographer Ron Cronin, who'd been photographing them. The three of us decided we imperatively had to go see what it looked like from closer than sixty miles away. But much of the mountain was still off limits; what was then called the Red Zone, the devastated and transformed areas of the east side and near the crater, was closed to all but authorized persons—scientists and loggers, mostly. We pulled a few governmental strings. We announced that we were artists with a selfless desire to record this historical event in pictures and words for posterity, etc., and they bit. We got a one-day pass into the Red Zone.

It was in October of 1981, sixteen months after the eruption, a gray day with a little rain on the wind. We set off at dawn but the car gave trouble, so we drove back to my house and got into our

VW bus and were off at last, first on I-5, then on the long road that goes up the west side of the mountain. That little old bus was a game one. Up from Cougar, Washington, the way deteriorated; nothing was using the high roads but log trucks, and around Windy Ridge we were on rocky, ashy ruts along hogbacks. There were no signs. There was nobody else on the mountain, except the loggers we could occasionally hear calling each other on the CB radio. We stayed too long, and the brief autumn dusk came down; we drove home in the dark. My husband was crazy with worry when we got home, after ten at night.

And it had been a long, scary day. But the fear I felt that day went deeper than the physical. After driving miles up through the endless green vitality of a great forest, to turn a corner and enter a world of grey ash, burnt stumps, and silence—from the complexity of flourishing life into the awful simplicity of death: the fear I felt then was metaphysical. And the scale of it all was beyond comprehension. I tried to write about it afterwards, in poetry and essay. I never felt I could describe it adequately, hardly hint at it.

And when I went back to the mountain twenty-five years later with the Foray, with people who hadn't seen the blast zone in those early years, I found there was no way to tell them what it had been like back then.

All slant, sloping dust: nothing standing but snags, burnt dead trees that had been stripped by the heat blast. Nearer the crater, whole hillsides of dead trees lying in strange patterns, toothpicks, blown down by the blast. And the total destruction area where there was nothing but ash hills, ash plains.

Little Meta Lake was a grey bit of murky water in a grey waste. Spirit Lake was a dirty foamy stinking brownish surface thick with floating dead trees. Everything smelled dead, a stink of burning and chemicals. Here and there, in a log-shadow or where a snowbank had been thick enough to protect seedlings before it was melted by the blast, we'd see a single tiny plant poking up through the dead grey-brown ash—pearly everlasting, vetch, fireweed—or a half-inch tree seedling, or one small mushroom: one at a time, and very few and far between. No birds. No beasts. Silence and ash. Grey slopes. Grey sky. The tiny bits of life too isolated and insignificant to offer anything but the hope of eventual renewal far in the future—a century, centuries. . . .

The destruction and desolation were almost impossible to take in, to comprehend. The mind offered similes: Hiroshima, Dresden; but this was not human-made. And not on a human scale at all. How to understand it?

Coming back a quarter of a century later, it was just as hard to comprehend that all that silent dead landscape was changed—was green—had come alive. Had always been alive. The paved highway we took to the Foray camp site and on to the other places we visited is the same awful road I drove with Henk and Ron. Again and again I saw the places we saw that day. The difficulty was in believing: *yes, this is it—this is the same place—that was the corner we turned from life to death.*

Wherever a ridge or hummock gave shelter from the blast, there are now groves of young silver fir, quite well grown, mixed with alder, willow, and shrubs (as well as some monoculture Douglas fir plantations where various interests insisted on "restoring the forest"). Grass meadows and grass slopes, streamside shrubs, and flowers everywhere—more Indian paintbrush than I ever saw anywhere, yellow oxeye daisies, blue lupine, the flame-colored native columbine, buckwheat, and yes—pearly everlasting, fireweed, vetch, not one tiny plant of each, but thousands and hundreds of thousands, hillsides of them, thick and lively, nodding in the wind. . . . Growth, vitality, wonderful variety—far more variety and exuberance than there had been in the dark second-growth canopy forest that was there before the eruption.

Only the pumice plain at the foot of the cirque-shaped crater is still lunar, pale, with huge dry channels and dusty plains. Beyond it is a weird landscape of big lumpy bits of mountain that fell northwest of the crater in the lateral eruption. If you know the landscape that I-5 goes through just north of Mount Shasta, the landforms are like that: strange random humps and hillocks, pieces of itself that Shasta has thrown around from time to time; it was amazing to see just such a landscape newly formed, still in process, taking shape.

Spirit Lake is fairly clear now and looks blue. The huge rafts of dead trees still float on it; they drift constantly with the wind, making strangely geometrical islands and continents. They are silvery, so it is quite pretty; although I heard a kid in a tourist group say to his mother, "I don't like that lake!"—which is, I believe, how the Indians always felt about Spirit Lake.

From Windy Ridge you look up into the crater. In 1981 it was full of steam, mist, and cloud, and I have no clear memory of what I saw then. On the Foray, our first visit, too, was on a rainy, cloudy day. But when we went next day we looked up through clear sunny air at the old dome, where the mountain first began to re-erect herself. She gave up that attempt some years ago, then began again in a different place. The new, growing dome is tucked up against the northwest wall, curiously like a young fetus in a womb; we could see only the very top of it, letting out peaceful wafts of steam. And we could see bits of the poor destroyed glacier, which they were just about to name when the new dome began heating up and melting it; I don't know if it ever got a name. And there is a fine waterfall, Loowit Fall, from the upper lip of the crater. Hot, they told us. A hot waterfall.

Much of the cognitive dissonance I was experiencing was explained and relieved by the scientists with us on the Foray. I listened to them with infinite pleasure. The main drift of what they said was this: We were absolutely wrong in every prediction we made after the eruption. They said this with jubilation. That is what is so lovable about real scientists: they rejoice in being proved wrong.

They said our mistake was to see this as destruction to be followed by a long slow restoration, whereas it was a process of sudden change and quick renewal, not merely going back to what it was, and not diminishing but enlarging the variety and energy of the biota of the mountain. They said, we thought the blasted and ashed areas would be colonized gradually from the outside, from the edges, and instead they were regrowing themselves within two years, often with unexpected species. They agreed that the gradient of this growth has been particularly steep the last two or three years—the mountain slopes have been greening themselves more and more quickly and thoroughly, just as in the past year the volcano has been building her new dome ceaselessly and energetically.

Mount St. Helens is a much better gardener than any logging company or government agency. Wherever we have succeeded in keeping human interference and exploitation out of the Monument, the renewal is on a broader scale than any "salvage" or plantings—more diverse, more vigorous, and more complete.

I wrote this poem about the view from our camp site.

> *From the tent on the volcano*
> The mist lifts off the little lake down there,
> Way down, across a gulf of shining air.
>
> The upward spiral song of Swainson's thrush,
> The white-crown's teedle-eedle in the hush:
>
> There is such singing in the morning, where
> Was only silence, and grey dust, and ash.
>
> "We are her children, we are in her care,
> Our kind destroyer," sings the mountain thrush.

Before we left on the Foray, anticipating the trip, I was extremely tense. I worried not only about coping with camping and hiking as a gimpy old crock, and living closely for four days with twenty-two strangers as a hopeless introvert, but also about the mountain—about going back up on the mountain. My previous visit had been magnificent, exhilarating, depressing, frightening, and stressful. And the Lady had not been at all quiet during the last few months. It was disquieting. . . . A constant earthquake series may become an earthquake swarm at any time, preceding cataclysm. The conduit that feeds lava up to the new dome is seven miles long—seven vertical miles—and what is going on down that deep in the Earth is absolutely unpredictable. It's one thing to watch a volcano sending out a great gorgeous sunlit plume of steam from sixty miles away, another thing to watch it seven miles from the crater. It's a long, long drive down off the mountain. . . .

But when I was there, getting ready to lie down and sleep on the volcano, any such thoughts and fears were entirely gone. I have no explanation. I guess I felt: well, now I'm here, I'm hers. I'm part of her, like all her trees and birds and lakes and dirt. So what she does I do, and that's OK. I never thought about it again.

Except when people made wisecracks, daring the mountain to "show her stuff"—then I would say, before I could stop myself, *Don't say that!* I meant it. It wasn't fear, or superstition, it was religion. You treat my Lady with respect!

Everyone was so kind and so good-natured and so interesting that I survived even having to be intellectually adequate at breakfast after waking up in a mud puddle. All I could possibly have wished for on the Foray was more silent time to sit and think and write or draw, but there was some of that each day, too. And always there was the summit above our camp, near, and always the faint breath of dust and vapor rising over it from the crater. I rise, says the mountain. I fall and rise.

Here is a poem I wrote a month or two before the Foray.

Another Weather: Mount St. Helens
Weightless clouds and airy rain drift over
a lower, slower weather in the world
where lava turns in vast typhoon pavanes,
thick fire beneath a ponderous earthen sky:

storms brew a thousand years before they break
in quaking thunder of tectonic shift
to hurl their hot bright hail straight up, send forth
the monstrous overwhelming wave, or still
a city into feathery clouds of glass.

I watch you, my volcano, through the depths
of sunlit air, and see you snowy-flanked
breathing your lazy steam-plume south, yourself
a vapor drifting, a bright veil of stone.

Change, Survival, and Revival: Lessons from Mount St. Helens

Charlie Crisafulli

When I arrived at Mount St. Helens shortly after the 1980 eruption, I was early in my career, a twenty-two-year-old half-trained ecologist, full of ambition and eager to learn all that the volcano offered. The offerings were large, and I was set on a journey now deep into its third decade, attempting to understand the ways the eruption impacted plants, animals, and fungi and their long-term responses to this disturbance. By now I've spent over fifteen hundred days in the field sampling biological populations throughout the volcanic landscapes, and hundreds of days more hiking, photographing, camping, skiing, and snowshoeing with family and friends. This work has been intellectually and physically exhilarating, while grounded in dust, grit, fatigue, and great camaraderie.

In order to really learn what nature has to teach, we have to immerse ourselves in the natural world and see it from the perspective of individual plants and animals. We have to get to know the whole cast of characters, pay detailed attention to their activities, and unravel the tangle of factors that influence them. Through this practice, this immersion in field observation, we can begin to understand the relationships among living organisms and their environment. It's also a way to explore how we, as humans, fit into the natural world.

Disturbance equals change, and disturbances like the 1980 eruption of Mount St. Helens are impetuous and vast. The initial eruption provoked awe, as a riot of geophysical forces was unleashed: hurricane-force, stone-filled winds; churning mudflows; super-hot, turbulent flows of frothy pumice; columns of ash and pumice blown high into the atmosphere. All these events, as profound and pervasive as they were, happened in half a day, a geologic instant, but set the stage for a longer, slower eruption—an eruption of life that would play out in a series of acts and scenes lasting centuries. The newly created biophysical stage provided unrivaled conditions for plants and animals—survivors and colonizers—to exploit these changes. Likewise it gave ecologists, myself included, unprecedented opportunities for studying how organisms initially respond to a complex ensemble of volcanic disturbance processes, and how the biological communities in forests, meadows, riparian areas, lakes, and streams are reassembled over the long term.

Survivors

For ecologists, the first order of business in the early days after the eruption was to determine if any organisms had survived, and if so, how many, where, and how. When we first flew over the landscape, we seriously doubted that any plant or animal had survived in the hardest-hit areas, but it quickly became clear that individuals of most, if not all, plant and animal species had survived at least in a few locations, and that survival was related to many different, often unexpected, factors. We were happy to see these survivors, but we questioned whether these plants and animals could persist under the new post-eruption conditions. This was an important question, because survivors embedded within these hard-hit zones could jumpstart recolonization of the disturbed area. Islands of survivors could be local sources of plants and animals, thus reducing the importance of dispersal from distant undisturbed areas and possibly speeding the pace of biological response. As it turns out, many, perhaps most, of the survivors persisted and played numerous and diverse ecological roles over the subsequent quarter century.

Colonists

Individual organisms that establish following a disturbance are called colonizers. At Mount St. Helens millions of individual plants and animals, representing thousands of species, have colonized since the 1980 eruption. They include all possible forms of life found in the larger landscape of the southern Washington Cascade Range: mammals, birds, amphibians, reptiles, fishes, insects and other invertebrates, fungi, plants of all sorts, and innumerable microbes. Individually and collectively they have increased the biodiversity and ecological complexity of the land and water, often at a stunning pace. Colonizers have played important roles in areas with survivors, but their presence is most noticeable where all life was obliterated by the eruption. With time many of these areas have transformed from barren rock to oases of verdant vegetation, rich with bird song, frog chorus, insect buzz, and wildflower scent.

Biological Community Development

For terrestrial environments, the first few years after the eruption was a period of modest growth and spread of survivors, and initial colonization of species. Each of these biological processes was severely restricted by the harsh environment (summer drought, high winds, poor soil conditions, low nutrients, absence of habitat), limited source populations, and limitations on their dispersal. But species did accrue over time, as more and more players gathered in the landscape. As time passed, surviving and colonizing plant populations grew, spread, and coalesced, filling gaps in the landscape. This created habitat for additional species, which in turn became further catalysts for colonization—riches begetting riches. With biological momentum increasing, species interacted in the whole array of trophic relationships: predator-prey, parasites, herbivory, seed dispersal, pollination, symbiosis!

Tales of a Survivor and a Colonizer

Each actor, each species, has a distinctive role in an ecosystem. In sparse ecosystems, such as those in the post-eruption landscape, certain roles are conspicuous and extremely important. I am particularly intrigued by the pocket gopher and lupine—an animal and a plant with powerful influence beyond their own kind.

Northern pocket gophers are small rodents with large forelimbs adapted for digging. They thrive in meadows and forest openings throughout the Cascade Range, non-forest habitats that are lush with the kinds of plants that have abundant below-ground plant parts favored by gophers. Their small eyes and ears, large incisors, and powerful forearms terminating in large claws make gophers very well suited for life below ground.

We suspected that gophers would survive the eruption because they would be protected beneath a mantle of soil. We conducted our initial surveys via low-level, bumpy, twisting helicopter flights. We flew back and forth, traversing slopes on the lookout for gopher burrows, dark mounds of organic soil against a uniform light gray pumice background. True to expectations, we discovered gophers surviving in many places, even in areas where all surface life had been wiped clean. Much like gophers, below-ground plant parts—roots, bulbs, corms, and rhizomes—had survived, continuing to provide nourishment for them. However, the long-term fate of the gophers was far from certain, because a long-term source of food was in question. Could the surviving plants send shoots up through the deep volcanic deposits in order to persist? Would new plants become established on the pumice surface quickly enough to offer a food source?

In many locations, deposits were initially too thick for plants to penetrate, but erosion removed some material, allowing plants to spring forth. In other locations, gophers facilitated the development of their own food supply. First, by their burrowing they loosened the soil and mixed it with pumice, easing the way for buried plants to send shoots upward. Second, by mixing the nutrient-poor pumice with the deeper pre-eruption, biologically rich soil, they created an ideal medium for seed germination and plant growth. In fact, we learned that more plants grew on gopher-modified soils than on adjacent pumice areas, and these plants grew larger and produced more flowers, fruits, and seeds. In later years, gophers' impacts were sometimes reversed: by creating chronic disturbance—churning and turning the soil—

they inhibited the development of complex plant communities in some locations.

The eruption and the changes it initiated created great opportunity for gophers. The blast-leveled forest transformed a vast landscape to "meadow," and gophers took advantage of the opportunity to spread far and wide. In doing so, they played many important ecological roles: by consuming plants or facilitating their growth, they altered the types, numbers, and distribution of plant species; they also created miles of tunnels with cool moist environments that could be used by amphibians and other animals to escape hot, dry surface conditions during the summer. Gophers reaped the benefit of the sudden transformation of the landscape for several decades, but with time, as forest cover returns, gophers will again be relegated to natural meadows and small forest openings. In the meanwhile, they reign superior.

The prairie lupine is a small, ground-hugging, short-lived (three to five years) evergreen plant of the Cascade-Sierra Nevada mountains that typically grows in poor soils on sunny, high-elevation, steep, wind-swept slopes. In this environment, with its short growing season, lupine plants "solar track," maneuvering their palmate leaves throughout the day, following the sun to efficiently harness the solar energy. They also minimize moisture loss by folding each leaflet when the air becomes too dry. Lupines have a special association, a partnership, with a bacterium on their roots—the plants provide the bacteria with simple sugars, used as a primary energy source, in exchange for nitrogen, thus enabling lupine to grow in nitrogen-poor soils.

Prairie lupines lived at and above timberline high on the slopes of Mount St. Helens before the 1980 eruption. During the eruption, a series of fiery-hot pyroclastic flows surged from the crater, severely disturbing an area immediately north of the summit. Before the eruption this area had been a cool, moist forest with mosses and ferns, shaded by majestic firs—poor habitat for lupines. The volcanic processes of 1980 transformed the area to a vast, sterile expanse of steaming rock and hissing fumaroles, dubbed the Pumice Plain.

My colleagues and I were very interested in documenting the development of life on this new landscape, and in 1981 we began aerial surveys from low-level helicopter flights. In June 1982 we were stunned to find a single adult lupine, ringed with its progeny, tiny lupine seedlings. We established a research plot around these few plants and monitored plant growth over the next twenty-six years. The lupine populations underwent dramatic boom-and-bust cycles, mediated by weather and a clan of insect seed-eaters, stem-borers, and leaf miners. Nonetheless, lupines played important roles by preparing the site for scores of other plant and animal species to colonize.

This sequence of events was possible because the new pumice plain environment created after the eruption mimicked alpine conditions where prairie lupine typically grows, albeit at a much higher elevation. Chance dispersal of a seed or plant fragment led to the establishment of that first lupine plant. Once established, lupine spread rapidly in this highly suitable and unoccupied landscape and set the stage for a wave of biological change. Lupines increased the carbon and nitrogen of the soil, provided litter that increased water retention, and snared seeds blown by wind, which collectively facilitated the colonization by dozens of other plant species. In turn these plants provided food and cover for numerous animals. Ironically, the changes made by lupine that enable other species to colonize and eventually dominate sites have decreased the suitability of the habitat for lupines. Eventually, other herbs, then shrubs, and finally trees will cover the plain, and lupine will gradually be pushed back up onto the upper flanks of Mount St. Helens, where they will remain until the next eruption.

Change, Nature, and the Human Lot

Dynamism is a pervasive theme in nature. The eruption caused sudden and dramatic change within a single day. Since that time characteristics of natural systems have changed as survivors grew and spread and other species colonized. Their populations waxed and waned, went through boom-and-bust cycles, species interacted, biological complexity increased, and communities underwent shifts in dominant species. The cadence of change has been fast during the first twenty-seven years since the big eruption, but will eventually slow, becoming barely perceivable, until, that is, another sudden dramatic event resets the clock.

The 1980 eruption of Mount St. Helens set in motion a succession of change for both nature and humans. Plants and wild animals as well as humans experienced survival and death, loss of habitat and home, destruction of dispersal corridors and roads. The initial survivors and colonizers, such as gophers and lupines, play important ecological roles during the first several decades and then wane in importance, yielding to the next group of organisms that dominate the scene. Similarly, scientists who arrived early in their career at Mount St. Helens in 1980 established permanent plot networks, conducted research for several decades, and will hand off the responsibilities to the next cohort of scientists.

During my twenty-seven years studying the ecology at Mount St. Helens, I have learned a great deal about how species and biological communities respond to change caused by volcanic disturbance. I have also thought hard about how we humans perceive disturbance, loss, and renewal. Long-term, committed work as a field ecologist has allowed me to become intimately familiar with a landscape and its inhabitants, and to better understand our relationship with nature. Ecologists like myself are colonists, of a sort. We tramp over extensive areas, set up sample plots, count organisms, and measure growth rates, while experiencing the landscape in every season and every kind of weather. What we record as scientific data is a very small sampling of a rigorous and plentiful life outdoors. And then we pass that sampling of knowledge on to others through the information web of science. Although we're just passing through, the science keeps accumulating, getting richer and more abundant, feeding more and more insights.

The Way to Windy Ridge

Tim McNulty

"I'm grateful to the mountain
because it gives me the opportunity to pray."
Ursula Le Guin

1.
We follow a high ridge
from Smith Creek headwaters
through crimson paintbrush
and healing stalks of fireweed,
> bright and tossing in the summer wind.

The white cymes of *Anaphalis:*
> "pearly everlasting"
flit and swirl pollyannish
> over this momentary landscape.

The first to come flocking back.

2.
The trail is cut through a blowdown fir,
wide rings of growth at its heart
sprung from an earlier disturbance
> —tephra fall or wildfire—
and dense rings of the outer edge
> marking centuries of quiet growth.

Then—
        one day.

Juncos say, "Same world, Tim."

3.
Below us, Spirit Lake is roofed
with a forest of drift logs.

Continents assemble
        and disassemble in wind,
collide and rift apart
as restless as the larger continents

           afloat
      on that warmer sea
               just beneath us.

4.
We skirt a palisade of lava cliffs,
remnant of an earlier flow.

Snags rise like Doric columns.
Loose rocks rumble and clack
to lakeshore;
puffs of ash float back up.

From a shallow ledge on the cliff face,
a delicate columbine blossom
        and wind-shook sprays of saxifrage
show us the way:

quiet exuberance
as the ground slips and rises beneath us.

5.
Around a final shoulder of ridge
the sloped expanse of Pumice Plain
        (drift of the mountain that stood before)
spreads into uneasy mesas
incised
        by shifting streams.

From a distance, the pale scrim of plant life
scrabbles wildly
                over the newly born ground,
        claiming every niche and corner.

6.
From the mile-wide bowl of the crater,
where dust and ash billow
from collapsing walls,
and an incipient glacier gathers itself,

the blessing of earthwarm water
spills through the blasted breach
                to a nascent greening earth

opaque with promise.

7.
We stand at a windy altar.
The volcano is washed in morning light.

Just out of sight,
a new lava dome heaves and falls,
swells at a pace that staggers.

The mountain is a window
                    open
        on the moment of creation.
From its ragged skirts
a fresh and hungry world unfurls.

Sinuous canyons, brushy slopes
and high windy ridges—
where we
                    for the moment
        enter into its story.

The view from here is more powerful,
daunting, yet flush with hope
                    for this damaged earth

than anyone dared imagine.

Part II

In Endless Song

Kathleen Dean Moore

1. *Ghost Lake*

Ghost Lake trail forges through the blast zone where the forest took the full force of the Mount St. Helens eruption. Spruce and fir lie where they fell, as if an army of trees, fleeing, had pitched on their faces in the direction of their flight. The blast rolled over them, scorched their limbs, crackled their skin, pressed them into the ash. Ranks on ranks of shattered tree trunks, half-buried in stones, reach out with broken limbs. The blast must have flanked the mountain and charged down the hillside, burning the slope to bedrock. Then the ground fell from under the trees, dropping them in a slag heap of pumice and slash. This is where we're hiking, my friends and I, across this grey and ruined land toward a pond pierced by snags.

My friends are singing. They astonish me. They laugh as they sing, dredging their memories for the words to an old hymn.

> *Through all the tumult and the strife*
> *I hear the music ringing.*

When I stop to listen, I am surprised to hear it too, the thin green pulse of frog song. A winter wren chatters in a huckleberry thicket, but I can't see it for all the leaves, and in fact a whole forest is growing from the ashes. Flocked with lichens, silver firs spiral toward blue sky. Chickadees flicker in the branches. Between the fallen trunks, fireweed and lupine grow lavishly purple and pink, blowsy with seeds. A golden-eye duck stands on one leg at the edge of the pond where my friend wades barefoot, waving her hand in time with the song.

It finds an echo in my soul—
How can I keep from singing?

What is this mountain, where hope rides the back of horror, the two of them galloping in such perfect synchrony that they might be one thing? The sorrow or the birdsong: which is the meaning of the mountain? In one second, only that, the blast seared the eyes of a robin who must have looked over her shoulder in sudden alarm. In the next second, everything was gone but her bones and the silence after the scream. Every bird killed. Every large mammal. Fifty-seven human beings. There are these facts. And not just these, but what they signify: that some day everything I love will be folded back into the Earth—that's how Scott Sanders said it. Every person I love, every song I sing, every beloved child, every poem will be folded back into the roar of Earth's fire and disappear forever.

At the same time, in the same place, there is the fact of fireweed. There is the fact of frogs returned, who knows how. Maybe they hopped through ashes or emerged, blinking, from mud under a snowbank behind a hill. There is the wandering coyote, kicking up dust as it licks for ants and defecates a twist of ash. There are the facts of spider silk tingling in green moss, and blanketing lichen, and beavers trooping down new rivercourses to chew willows nourished by elk born in ash and dust. There must be a lesson here too, and is it this?—that no matter how fragile and finite small lives may be, no matter how we grieve foresight of our own deaths, Life itself is a powerful force that will not be turned away. But how can we take comfort in that, we mortals who cling to the significance of small lives?

2. Horse Ridge

We've pitched our tents in pumice on a north-south spine. Snow-crowned Mt. Adams floats on forests to the east; to the west, Mount St. Helens stands raw and grey. As daylight drains off our camp, pink light collects in the cracked bowl of the volcano. One by one, we set down our coffee cups and gather on the ridge to watch. The pink cloud glows above lavender cliffs and dims the rosy distance. At a sudden rumble of rock, we shout and scramble for binoculars to watch rubble roll down the caldera's flank. A dust plume boils up, bursts red, and pulses over the rim. The last of the light shafts through broken rock, flickering in the smoke.

I've seen paintings of Creation that look like this—a red gleam moving over smoking stone. And I've seen imaginings of the end of time that look just the same—gray rock seamed with fire, rising smoke, falling darkness, nothing left of life except a handful of human beings lined up at the edge of Destruction, unable to speak.

The smoke stays with me in my dreams. In the dark before morning, low rumbling shakes me awake. Light strobes the side of the tent. An eruption? I'm on my knees at the door. But it's lightning that crashes between the mountains. Thunder rolls again, and I unzip the tent. The broken side of the mountain, that shattered tooth, fills the doorway. A bolt of lightning shoots from the crater almost to the moon, half hidden behind glowing clouds. The tent fills with light. Thunder shakes the ground under my knees. Should I run down the road to the landing and bring up a van to protect them, all the beautiful, pyroclastic minds of my friends?

One. Two. Three. I count the seconds to gauge the distance of the storm and turn my head to judge its direction. Making camp on the highest ridge for miles around had seemed like such a good idea. The lightning might pass to the north. It might not.

In the morning, I pull on a rain slicker and climb out into a cold, wet day. Dawn floods under purple clouds that dash lightning onto the mountains to the north. Wind-driven rain rivers down the road. But sunshine pours over clouds on Mt. Adams, and when we gather for breakfast, a meadowlark sings.

Under the flapping tarp that shelters the picnic tables, a geologist is hanging onto the tent poles to keep the whole structure from winging across the valley. With his free hand, he gestures toward the crater. "Lightning creates the conditions for life," he says. "The gas cloud over the 1980 eruption was full of lightning—up, down, every which way. The lightning charged the nitrogen in the ammonia and ozone. So when the ash finally fell from the cloud, it was full of the nitrogen that would fertilize new plants." Here on the volcano, I no longer understand the difference between destruction and creation.

The scientists among us can hardly contain their excitement at the ecological possibilities of the eruption, what they call this great "biomass disturbance event." Disturbance kicks the world into motion. What had been stagnant, the mature stands of fir and pine, is booted into new life. What had been simple is now complex. What had been monochrome is now a hillside of purple lupine and orange butterflies. What had been silent now chatters and sings.

Destruction, creation, catastrophe, renewal, sorrow, and joy— these are human projections onto the landscape, the ecologists say. What is real, they say, is change. What is necessary, they say, is change. Suddenly, there are new niches, new places to grow and flourish—ponds, landslides, rocky hillsides, a great profusion of edges where beetles troop over stumps, huckleberries emerge from snowbanks, astonished pocket gophers dig into the sun. Between the forest patches, meadows fill with the creatures of wet prairies and oak savannahs.

"Meadowlarks!" an ecologist exults, sweeping his arm toward the expanse of lupines and corn lilies under the storm. "Where else can you find meadowlarks on a mountaintop?"

This biomass disturbance has made a new place for birdsong. I understand that. But at what terrible cost to nestlings burned in their nests, the sudden silence where there had been hungry peeping? Lord knows, I'd like to see the world the way ecologists do. If all of us thought of death as change rather than catastrophe, could we blunt Earth's edge of sorrow? And isn't this a source of hope, that the forces of nature turn death into life again and again, unceasing?

Above Earth's lamentation,
I hear the sweet though far-off hymn
That hails a new creation.

But sometimes I can't hear the hymn for the crying of small birds in the back of my mind.

3. *The Trail from Donnybrook*

Climbing the trail from Donnybrook, I take small steps across a landscape of falling, this mountain in the process of falling down. It scares me to walk the trail, one jogging shoe on a rock that must only yesterday have fallen from the mountain, the other on a slope of pumice that trickles down the hill. If I slip, there is nothing that will hold me. The little flower called pearly everlasting clings to the rubble by what roots? By what hope against reason? And how can it deserve this name—everlasting— with one root in dribbling rubble, the other under a new-fallen stone?

Putting one foot in front of the other across this scratch in the cliff, I lift my hand to block the view of the distance below me to Spirit Lake. The lake lies as still as the silence after a car wreck—that still, except for floating tree trunks, bare and grey. They slowly rotate in the wind that curls around the cliff. How do we walk these skidding paths across the edge of an Earth that is tumbling around us? I can hear it go — the clink of cobbles down the face of rough stone. Every step spills sand and stone and bends fireweed to the ground.

I thought I would learn peace from the mountain. Acceptance. I thought I would find comfort in the tenacity of life precariously rooted in constant change. I thought I would learn grace, which is only this: balance as the world slides away under my feet. Instead, I learned how different I am from a mountain, which is not afraid to fall.

Tumbling rocks shake me, body and soul. Cascading down, leaping over rimrock, filling the valleys, the stream of pebbles shakes the belief that human lives are the measure of time. They undercut the conceit that humans are the center of creation, our hopes and sorrows a special concern of the Earth's. And what do they say about human pride, the confidence that global events are under human control, that we might understand and dominate the Earth? *Ha.* The mountain laughs. *Ha,* a great explosion of ash and steam, jolted by lightning.

But then there is this: Would we fear loss so desperately, if we didn't have such a love for the Earth and its life, for our own lives in the midst of indifferent laughter? Would we be afraid of the silence of a robin, if a robin's song didn't mean so much to us? Would we be so afraid of our own deaths, if we didn't love life so urgently? Maybe fear of losing it all can lead us to a place of rejoicing, a recognition of how deeply we value the living, changing world, how lovingly we cling to our place in it.

How should a person live in a world that erupts catastrophically, sliding down and down? On the flank of this big volcano we call Earth, how should a person live? I don't know for sure. But this, at least, is important: Especially when I'm afraid, to be open to wonder. Especially when I'm grieving, to be amazed by beauty. To rejoice at the inevitability of change and the urgency of life, the power of the Earth that flows out from its center and gathers all life back into its fold. And especially when I'm caught up in my human-scaled sense of time and significance, to remember that my life is part of the endless flow of fiery rock. To be astonished and grateful. *My life flows on in endless song,* the hymn says. *How can I keep from singing?*

Volcanic Blues; or, How the Butterfly Tamed the Volcano

Robert Michael Pyle

An old tale from somewhere around the Pacific Rim of Fire relates how a village was threatened by a fierce volcano. The People importuned the volcano spirit, but she only puffed more steam and ash at them. Eagle and Raven also appealed to the volcano to spare the village and the forest, but the volcano rebuffed them too. They flapped raggedly back down the mountain, singed and covered with ash, and shrugged. Finally, a mere butterfly fluttered up the long steep slopes to the volcano's crater and delivered her own petition in her tiny voice. This time the volcano heard, and giving Butterfly time to get out of the way first, promptly erupted. She spared the village, but leveled about half of the forest. Butterfly was happy, for she knew that without a good eruption now and then to clear the deep, dark forest, the meadows and sunny slopes that her kind needed would cease to exist. Eagle and Raven and People had only asked for safety; Butterfly had asked for renewal.

Or if there is no such tale, there ought to be.

꙳ ꙳ ꙳

In eastern Washington and throughout the arid West there occurs a group of small blue butterflies known as the dotted blues (genus *Euphilotes*). Well under an inch in wingspan, the males of these rapid-flying mites are pale to deep blue above, the females mole-brown or gray, both chalky white below and peppered with the black dots of their name. Bright lunules, pale orange-juice to fire-engine red, line the rim of the hind wings on both sides. All *Euphilotes* depend solely upon species of buckwheat (*Eriogonum*) for their larval host plants. We've long believed we had two species of these butterflies in Washington, assigned to *E. battoides* (the square-spotted blue) and *E. enoptes* (the western dotted blue). But in recent years, with close study of host plant relationships and DNA, the picture is growing more complicated. It seems that particular species of blues have evolved in intimate (and obligate) association with not just buckwheats in general, but specific types of buckwheat, and we have more kinds of blues than we thought.

The Washington species long assigned to *E. enoptes* has turned out to be *E. columbiae*, the Columbia blue, formerly regarded as a subspecies. Lepidopterists Dave Nunnalee and David James, one a dedicated amateur, the other a state entomologist, have been rearing all of the butterflies resident in Washington. They have found that the pillbug-sized caterpillars of Columbia blues exploit northern buckwheat (*Eriogonum compositum*) early in the flight season, then use the later-flowering tall buckwheat (*E. elatum*) as summer progresses. The larvae tend to match the colors of the flowers they graze, appearing pinker or creamier depending on their chosen buckwheat. The true *Euphilotes enoptes* seemed to be restricted to California and Oregon, feeding on bare-stemmed buckwheat (*Eriogonum nudum*), which looks like a small version of *E. elatum*. Andrew Warren, of the McGuire Center for Lepidoptera and Biodiversity in Gainesville, Florida, is another of the lepidopterists who has been figuring all this out. When a graduate student at Oregon State University, Andy urged butterfly folk north of the Columbia to try to locate *Eriogonum nudum* in Washington; if we could do so, he thought, we might well find the actual *Euphilotes enoptes* also, as a new species for the state.

Loving this sort of a challenge, my botanist wife, Thea, and I tracked down the known records for bare-stemmed buckwheat. There were only two in the University of Washington herbarium, and a couple of others in separate databases, including one from a Washington Native Plant Society foray to the Dark Divide, east of Mount St. Helens, that we'd actually been along on. Come spring, we found the Yakima County site for the plant that has been recorded by our old U.W. mentor, Art Kruckeberg. There was the buckwheat, in tight, pink bud and cold, wet rain: no butterflies, to be sure. But a fortnight later the bloom was out, crowding the roadcuts above the deep canyon with creamy little flowers on their smooth green stalks. Crossing the road we whooped with joy, as minute flickers of azure gave away the newest-known member of the Washington butterfly fauna.

We would see many dotted blues that day, all *E. enoptes*, most of them nectaring or laying eggs on their rare host plant. But were there any more, elsewhere? The other *E. nudum* record from the U.W. herbarium was an old one from an unspecified location in the Goat Rocks Wilderness Area, west of where we'd found the plant and its butterfly. We hiked into likely habitat in fog so thick it might have been shed by the eponymous goats. The only buckwheat to be seen was the cushion species known as *E. pyrolifolium* for its leaves, shaped like those of pears. We searched further, as did Dave Nunnalee and others. Only a few patches of the plant turned up, near White Pass. It began to seem as if the plant might be as rare as the lack of records suggested, and the butterfly just as limited.

        ‡ ‡ ‡

It was the middle of July, and a pack of scientists and writers gathered for several days of camping, hiking, jawboning, eating, drinking, and storytelling on the slopes of Mount St. Helens. A little late arriving, I was taking the curves of Forest Road 99 with some celerity. A few miles short of the meeting place, I rounded the thirty-third curve or so and took in the spectacle of an entire slope of what looked for all the world like bare-stemmed buckwheat. "*What?*" I said. Then, braking hard, followed up with "Holy shit!" It must be pearly everlasting, I told myself. That redoubtable native plant upholsters vast areas of the blast zone, and it is not entirely dissimilar, at speed, from my nudie cutie. But when I pulled over and got a good look, there was no doubt: this was *Eriogonum nudum* —lots of it!—blooming weeks later at this higher elevation than in our Yakima County location, though most clusters had blossomed by now, with still a few pink buds to go. Between the point where the plant kicked in and the turnoff to the camping site, I saw acres of it, if the verges and cuts had been flattened out: vanilla drifts against the milky white ash.

I wondered how the plant could be so abundant here, in one of the most-studied ecosystems in Washington, and yet so rare in the herbaria and lists? Around our campfire that night, I put the question to Charlie Crissafulli, Forest Service ecologist for Mount St. Helens National Volcanic Monument. Charlie told me that he knew the plant well, but hadn't appreciated its rarity in Washington outside the monument. His theory was that it had come in on road-building material during post-eruptive construction. That seemed plausible on first consideration, since bare-stemmed buckwheat loves well-drained, disturbed slopes such as roadcuts. From there it might have spread out into ashfields. However, given the plant's spotty (to put it generously) distribution in the state, the chances of a gravel source containing its seeds or roots seemed highly unlikely to me. Besides, as I would see later, the buckwheat was so well established along so many miles, and so far beyond the road margins, that such a degree of spread in the years since the roads were rebuilt seemed equally improbable. But the question also seemed moot: how could you know?

Given our schedule and the deteriorating weather, my chances to look for buckwheat blues didn't look good. The third day began with wild weather and a cold, saturated wind like the drooling howl of some deep-sea beast. The company split up into groups depending on which of several possible hikes they favored. Two of us, Ursula Le Guin and I, opted instead for a general look around at a number of sites. Fred Swanson, consummate forest ecologist and visionary who strongly believes in the happy meeting of art and science, kindly accommodated our whim. He drove us to Windy Ridge, Meta Lake, and a number of viewpoints in between, sharing history in deep and recent time as few could. Ursula pointed out this declivity, that prominence that caught her eye, and that we could well imagine she had invented out of the mist. Fred showed why he loves the place so damn much. I spotted the odd wind-tossed bird. We had a ball. Then we headed way up north along the Green River to the far edge of the monument, hearing the history of forests felled by architectonic forces and chain saws, the latter fortunately arrested before their all-too-obvious lines pushed any farther upvalley.

I'd noticed plenty of the buckwheat on the way up the Green River road. And then, on the way back down, lo! The sun came out! Fred said there was time for me to have a look, so I hopped out of the car and made my awkward way up the loose pumice slope between bleached "driftwood" and pearly everlasting, taking care not to step on the buckwheats blooming among them, but swishing them with my net bag to put up any insects stirred by the latent sun. A quick flitter that might have been a small, gray female blue was more likely a fly. But then there was a definite blue flash, big and bright. I'd disturbed it from a buckwheat head. The butterfly rose over me, then dropped downslope to another cluster, where it settled and commenced to nectar. I moved that way, trying to keep my footing. But the unstable substrate crumbled, threatening to disturb the butterfly. I could see that my best chance would be a controlled fall, or a targeted plummet. I leapt, swinging my net as I passed the blue, then flipped it over and turned my attention to landing upright on the road below. I made it, and I had the butterfly. Ursula later told me that she watched my abrupt descent of the steep ash-pitch with a combination of amusement and considerable alarm. Gratifying *wow*s escaped Ursula and Fred as they viewed the brilliant, foil-blue wings of my quarry. Then they left me to walk the buckwheat verges and ravines down to the main road, flicking my net. But the day cooled again, and I saw no more blue, either above or on the wing.

☙ ☙ ☙

The insect I'd caught was not a dotted blue; it wasn't even a true blue. Though *Lycaena heteronea* males flash the deepest, most shimmering cerulean of any of our blue butterflies, this species actually belongs to a related group of lycaenids (gossamer wings) known as coppers. This we know from its wing veins, genitalia, and other structural traits. Twice the size of a dotted blue and silvery white below, the blue copper closely resembles the fiery bronze copper (*L. rubidus*) except in color: mere hue, whether pigmented or prismatic as in these iridescent gems, can evolve rapidly, while structure is much more stable over time. But like the genus *Euphilotes*, and unlike most other coppers (which tend to develop on docks, *Rumex* species), the blue copper feeds solely on species of buckwheat as a caterpillar. In this case, it must have been using *E. nudum*. The only other species of buckwheat known to occur in the monument, *E. pyrolifolium*, grows on high, blast-protected outcrops of the mountain, subalpine habitats such as in the Goat Rocks, and blue coppers, chiefly resident east of the Cascades in dry habitats, are not known to employ that species. This was the first record of the blue copper in Skamania County, and the first occurrence well west of the Cascade Crest, a range extension of some forty miles. While some butterflies are mobile, quickly colonizing new territory, they tend to be generalists with widespread, weedy food plants. In contrast, *L. heteronea* is a sedentary host plant specialist, seldom found far from the nearest buckwheat.

The surprising discovery of blue coppers at Mount St. Helens allows us to make an educated guess about the source of the mystery buckwheat on the monument. Even if *E. nudum* had indeed come in with road gravel, the chances of copper eggs or larvae coming with it, or a gravid female copper finding it there, seem vanishingly small. Parsimony suggests that both the plant and the butterfly were there in the first place, and survived the eruption of 1980. More than survived: in the case of the bare-stemmed buckwheat, at least, absolutely thrived. Supposing it was present but restricted before (as the lack of records suggests), the post-eruptive conditions—thousands of acres of new, dry, hot pumice slopes much like the gravelly screes and roadcuts this plant loves—allowed a rapid adaptive spread known as "ecological release." The blue copper has presumably advanced with it.

Further sunny, summer sampling bore this out. The following summer I found a female blue copper at the Clearwater interpretive overlook, and yet another buckwheat-feeding species, the acmon blue (*Plebejus acmon*) along the Green River. *Euphilotes enoptes*, the western dotted blue, has not yet turned up on the Monument, but we'll continue to look for it. Its occurrence there along with the other two buckwheat butterflies would cinch the case for *E. nudum* predating the eruption at Mount St. Helens. Perhaps, in the right season and weather, this "new" Washington butterfly will swarm over waving fields of buckwheat on Loowit.

I am a biogeographer, and the distribution of plants and animals—why they occur here, why not there—is of infinite interest to me. But there are larger implications here than dots on a map. By chance, I conducted the last butterfly sampling on the mountain prior to her 1980 eruption. While I found a nice array of butterflies near the former Timberline campground— snowberry checkerspots and northern blues in abundance, a few others—the diversity (as one would expect in a young alpine habitat) wasn't high. And then almost all that habitat, I thought, was scarified by the blast. Subsequent surveys have found that all the species I'd tallied in 1979 have recovered, but have noted few others. So I had long believed that Mount St. Helens had little to offer in the way of butterfly surprises.

Then in the fall of 1997, Thea and I found American painted ladies prolific on Johnson Ridge. Though its larvae feed on the widespread pearly everlasting, *Vanessa virginiensis* is a distinctly uncommon butterfly in the state. Conditions here on the pumice desert must have proved perfect for both species, the ladies abounding on a blanket of everlasting. Since then, Charlie Crissafulli has found Edith's checkerspot larvae defoliating Cardwell's penstemons on barren-looking Windy Ridge. And then the blue copper. Clearly, more life survived the eruption than I'd expected, a fact I've heard over and over from the scientists. And just as clearly, Loowit holds out more potential for butterfly discovery than I had guessed.

We know other examples of Cascadian butterflies not only favored by periodic vulcanism, but actually evolving in concert with the volcanic landscape. The "sand plains" left behind by the ash-plume of massive Mount Mazama's great blow, east of its surviving caldera, known as Crater Lake, have long been recognized as harboring a distinctive fritillary butterfly. This was finally named *Speyeria egleis moecki* for its discoverer, Arthur Moeck, by Paul Hammond and Ernst Dornfeld in 1983. And then in 1995, veteran lepidopterist Harold Rice discovered a truly minuscule blue on a truly tiny buckwheat on the same Mazama ashfields. Hammond and Dave McCorkle named it *Philotiella leona* for Harold's wife and collecting partner, and I designated it Leona's little blue in *The Butterflies of Cascadia*. *P. leona* is almost invisible as it darts over the sandy flats, both the summer air and the pyroclastics nearly as hot as when Mazama erupted.

What else might be lurking in these vast and challenging fields of fire? What butterflies—not eradicated, but rather renewed, have proliferated, even evolved through this natural act of so-called destruction? And what would the giant copper mine proposed for Goat Mountain, up the Green River just outside the monument, mean for the butterflies and their buckwheats? If I were the mining boss, I would watch out for that tiny butterfly. This is a longer, more complicated version of that old tale about the volcano and the butterfly; but the moral is the same.

Mount St. Helens

John Calderazzo

—after twenty-five years

Before it blew in 1980 I had never heard of it
never seen it from an airplane or high ridge
a tremendous bell of rock & snow
ringing with noonday light
drawing miles of forests
to attention.
Only later
did I see the photographs
the years of dawns & dusks
its Fuji summit glowed bright pink
a paper lantern floating over clouds
as though its secret heart of fire
had been blazing all that time.

Many-named volcano
Loowit Smoke Mountain St. Helens.
And who was Helen?
Saint of Burning Stone
pluming up through crust glaciers sky?
Holy Mother of Earth dreaming of new earth?

A tower of pumice & ash twelve miles high
blackened that rattling Sunday morning
full of sun
while half a country east
I nursed a breakfast hung over most likely
& unaware that rocks could boil & fly

that the planet could regrow itself
from its own burning core
over and over.

Those days
I lived in gray weather
I hardly saw the ash ferried through
Cascades Rockies rolling Great Plains skies
to the flat farms of northwest Ohio
fine deep-Earth moon flakes
misting down on
their circling of the globe
as I churned
through Rita Joanie Whoever
cracking myself open I told myself
but giving off such stingy light.

If only I'd known
the basement philosophy of volcanoes
that sooner or later everything comes unstuck
& moves in a deep time stew
convecting beyond my life your life
beyond evacuation
& life of country or culture
except for the culture
of constant change & renewal.
Maybe that volcano dust began to work
on me.

Easy to talk about myself I realize
so far from the giant blow-down forests
that pinned the dead
though not anyone I knew
not even a landscape
I knew well enough to mourn

blasted in seconds into miles & decades
of moonslope
four-foot-thick shattered trees
that men & women I have since met
vowed to protect with their science
to nurse through illness
their hearts
still bruised after twenty-five years
though who could have stopped
that fast forward pestilence
flattening Douglas firs
in Sasquatch- & owl-haunted shadows
& Spirit Lake so quickly gorged
with everything but blue water?

When the bulge broke
the mountain became mythology.
Snow flashed to steam
& frozen soil to scalding mud.
Torrents choked with boulders
swelled the North Fork of the Toutle
with upturned elk boiled fish
something I never want to see
again said a man I met this year
baiting a hook along that river
as Loowit smoked again
though mildly.
But when the top & flank
blew off the mountain
the wet concrete current
took a house & slammed
it into a bridge
two stories torn neatly open.
On video a half-house spills
a bed a couch a fridge.

The Earth can ruin you with its riches
vaults flung open to free
a glowing avalanche
a stone wind stabbed by lightning
Spirit Lake still clogged
with tree trunks whitening like bones
floating & shifting by the century
or the rippled millisecond
the long & short
of terrestrial evolution
mindquakes that make you yammer
against God buried fire the split personality
of the planet.

Or sob with hope
because Saint Helen
at least the Swedish martyr Helen of Skofde
was launched in a stone coffin
that refused to sink
that spawned a healing spring
wherever it bumped ashore.
And elk now crowd Loowit valleys.
And soil that dropped sizzling from the sky
cooled then cupped the seeds
that wandered in
on long shoulders of wind
or pushed up as shoots
of pearly everlasting Noble fir fireweed.

Packed down shields of devastation
loosened & finally opened
to the sun
as I have since then
having learned to slow down
& travel far

having learned
to sit in the new light
of this Smoke Mountain & others
Mont Pelée Soufriere Hills
Redoubt Vesuvius Etna
which let me watch & feel
how time's snapped bones re-knit
how so many kinds of gray
can turn green.

On the Ridge

Robin Kimmerer

I come from a green and gentle place of dairy farms in the mapled hills of upstate New York. We don't lock our doors and the kids still play in the woods and grow up knowing how to run a tractor. I know the names of most of the folks whose lights I can see across the valley. The ancient rocks beneath the apple trees were molten once, but this is a landscape shaped by ice, not by fire. In this old land, worn smooth by the palm of the glacier, my consciousness had no room for volcanoes.

So with eyes accustomed to soft green hills, I was unprepared for the close-up experience of Mount St. Helens, let alone camping on her flanks. It wasn't always that way. I'd come here before, just the year after the 1980 eruption, and viewed the new geography with the detachment of a scientist from the safe distance of the Visitors Center across the valley. This time was different. I brought something with me that I hadn't known back then. I came to witness this landscape a quarter century after the eruption, only to find that I could barely look at it. Too terrible to look at, too beautiful to look away. The size and power of the blasted land rolled over me like the shockwave that had vaporized the land. I found that looking directly at the steaming mountain made me weak with a visceral desire to run fast and run far. I swallowed hard and could bear only a sideways glance at her looming presence, the crater like an all-seeing eye. I felt like a kid with my hands over my eyes, trying to preserve the illusion that if I couldn't see the destroyer, then it couldn't see me.

I found respite in the familiar perspective of looking at the ground. The story of destruction was written in slashes of raw red rock, but the story of creation was written in small, leafy script. Looking close, I found individual shoots of moss growing

41

from the pores in a pumice pebble, like miniature hanging gardens. Clumps of grass struggled in the lee of a shattered rock and lupines blossomed over the ash. I was comforted by green.

The scientists among us reassured us that "an event"—geologists' shorthand for eruption—was most unlikely, but that was small comfort. I usually like to camp in solitude, but this time I pitched my tent near to others. If this mountain were to blow again, I wanted a hand to hold. I've always known that my demise could come at any moment, but sleeping on an active volcano seemed to tempt the fates. I looked out at the mountain, so close, so powerful, a puff of steam hanging over the jagged place where the summit had once stood strong and secure. As I lay in my sleeping bag, I thought of my daughters. I knew I could die here. With hips dug into tephra hurled to this very spot on a superheated wind of suffocating gases, sleep came slowly. I heard a rumble. Maybe it was an airplane. Maybe not. So I zipped my tent.

Eyewitnesses to the blast describe the immediate aftermath as the world transposed like a photographic negative. What was lush and green became gray, what had been up was down; convex became concave, presence became absence, and every hint of color was lost in a blanket of deep gray ash. Only memory was not erased, memories of a serene and snowy cone, skirted by moss-draped forest and fragrant with the smell of humus, moist and earthy. Trout streams, waterfalls, glittering lakes, all vaporized in a searing blast so dramatic as to cauterize grief and leave only awe.

Within days of the blast, scientists helicoptered in to witness the destruction. But at the heart of the devastation, they also found the forces of creation. With ash still hot beneath their boots, they watched the process of how land begins again. The spiders were the first to arrive, ballooning in on gossamer strands, as if to reweave the blasted earth with silk. Apparently, the air is always full of floating spiders, but we only take notice when everything else is gone. Scientists expected that the recovery would occur in just this way, from a living rain of propagules flying in from outside like the proverbial dove with an olive branch that signaled the resurgence of life. Indeed, biologists have measured a steady inflow of microbes, seeds, insects, and birds on the wind. The first arrivals had nothing to sustain them and perished upon landing in the ash. Most could not survive, but still they came like a rain of promises. The tiny gardens that had drawn my eyes were the product of this hopeful rain, life trying to heal itself with green.

Ecologists predicted that it would be many decades until green came again to cover the pumice-gray and brick-red crags of baked earth. But they were wrong. It wasn't decades, or even years. To everyone's surprise, the first greening of the ash did not come from outside, but from within. In a matter of days, the ashy crust began to rise and bend and crack itself open, much as the earth had done just a few days before. But the subterranean forces that buckled the ash crust were not born in magma—they were ferns, wanting to live. The eruption that had changed almost everything hadn't changed the fact that it was spring. The ferns didn't know what had happened; last year's buds were waiting below ground, tightly coiled. The deep soil had protected them and, called by spring, the primordial curls of fern fiddleheads pushed their long way up through the ash and broke through to sunlight. What a surprise they must have had on that morning in May, to emerge to the absence of forest. But, faithful to the spring, they unfurled their leaves and made a place for spiders to land, tiny islands of green in the desolation of gray.

Scattered here and there on the plains of destruction were many such refugia, tiny islands of survival that had been spared incineration by the sheer happenstance of place and time. Life itself is so improbable, and on that May morning, so was survival. Where a late snowbank still lay in a hollow, the ground beneath was insulated from the searing blast and seedlings grew. Where ice was thick on a pond, the water did not boil completely away and a few zooplankton remained to restart the food web. Improbable, lucky, and essential to recovery. Scientists were surprised by the regenerative power of these tiny specks on a barren wasteland and called them "biological legacies." These scraps of the former forest played a vital role in recolonizing after the blast, and they produced a more rapid rate of recovery that anyone had predicted. Forest ecologist Jerry Franklin said that in terms of recovery after destruction, "it wasn't what was lost that mattered, but what was left behind." Observers of the recovery learned that healing of the land began from inner resilience. Without the biological legacies to sustain life, the rain of seeds and spiders from outside would have been impotent.

In the next days, our band of writers hiked further into the blast zone, always coming closer and closer to the crater. I squinted into the harsh July light to see the braided patterns of recovery where grasses grew and seedling firs had established. Still I could not hold the gaze of the mountain. I was glad when the trail took us onto the backside of a ridge, whose shadow gave respite from the sun and the unblinking eye of the crater. In this welcome shelter from its looming presence, I could breathe more easily and begin to see again.

Most all was bare, but for a thatch of new grasses and some shrubs taking hold. The narrow trail followed the contours of the land and dipped into an old gully. Sheltered by the barest crease in topography, here the skeleton of a single tree had been spared. On the leeside of the hard and silvered trunk was a knothole, a damp depression that had faced away from the blast. And in the knothole was a vibrant (grateful?) clump of moss, the most heartfelt green that I'd seen for days. I looked closer, and saw that this was not just any moss, but *Antitrichia*, whose native home was the shady richness of old-growth forest. Because there was not another tree or moss for miles, I knew that this was no recent colonist borne on the wind. This was a biological legacy, a moss that had been sheltered by the knothole, which had been guarded by the tree, which had been protected by the gully, which has been shielded from the blast by the hill. And sprouting from the fist-sized moss garden was a tiny fern. A survivor that would one day ensure the return of moss-draped firs. Life persists and perishes this way, protected by layers and layers of chance.

It was then that I heard it, the dry trickle of pebbles as the pumice beneath my feet began to slip away. In fast-moving runnels, the hill was beginning to move. There was nothing but gravity between me and Spirit Lake, hundreds of feet below. Carefully, carefully I moved forward so as not to disturb the rest of the slope. I had felt safer out of the gaze of the searching eye, but even here destruction hovered, whether I would look at it or not. There is no such thing as safety. The path ahead became a crumbling ledge and all my instincts for preservation of life and limb boiled over to head-swimming vertigo. I could not make myself go on. Only with the steadying hand of a friend was I able to make the traverse, a walk between wonder and abject terror.

At last, the path led us out of the shadow. The crater gaped before us, a living, breathing force I could smell and taste on the air, like the sulfurous blowhole of the earth. This landscape would not let me take cover behind denial of what I feared most. I felt myself surrender to its truth. And so I looked straight on into the crater where the earth shook with its own transformation. The steaming vents and rockfalls sent up dust plumes to mingle with the iridescent gas clouds. I sat silent among the lupines, mesmerized by the bulging lava dome, and my thoughts were drawn to home.

I had thought there was safety in my green hamlet among the apple trees. I did not know that even there magma was forcing its way to our midst, even as I was packing my bags for Mount St. Helens. The eruption came on a soft June morning, when the pastures were rich with promises and the honeysuckle had just come into bloom. It was a day we all looked forward to—a tradition in our town in which Holsteins outnumber people. Tractor Day. In a celebration of who we are, the high-school kids drive their tractors to school, and the parking lot fills with old John Deeres, a red FarmAll, combines and lawn mowers. They come from all over the hills and converge in a caravan down

Main Street. But, this year there was one who did not make it; a laughing boy coming down a steep hill on his father's old Massey Ferguson. Mike, the sweet-faced son of the school-board president and the fourth-grade teacher died when his tractor rolled on top of him in a thicket of honeysuckle, so fragrant on that spring morning. To perish or persist depends on so little, layers upon layers of chance.

Grief erupted in a pyroclastic flow that engulfed our town. His parents' faces became too terrible to look at, too beautiful to look away. In just a moment, our soft green life became a blast zone, a scalded pumice plain. We drew together, like tents on a windy ridge to face the unthinkable. We offered each other hands to hold as the trail crumbled away. We held our children tighter. But for the shelter of happenstance, we knew it could have been us instead. Whether we deny it or not, there is no such thing as safety. We could die here. And so we gathered in the overflowing church to sing; "Was blind but now I see."

We showered the family with calls and cards and food. But we know that these kindnesses are like the impotent rain of spiderlings and seeds upon the burned earth of their grief. The mountain says that recovery does not come from outside, but from within. It is what is left behind that matters. Where does healing come from? I've seen fiddleheads come up through ashes, but I don't know how.

That night I looked out my tent door at the mountain, steaming pink in the moonlight. And I thought once again—I could die here. And I thought, too, that I could live. Together, we gather on the ridge between creation and destruction. What else can we do, but stand in the moonlight and sing?

In the Zone: Notes from Camp

Tony Vogt

> *The way you can go*
> *Isn't the real way.*
> *The name you can say*
> *Isn't the real name.*
> —Lao Tzu, Tao Te Ching (translation by Ursula Le Guin)

When I first encountered Mount St. Helens, I was bewildered. Knowing her through tales of Sasquatch and images of ashen eruption, I had expected a mountain of mystery and cataclysm. Yet my first impression was otherwise. On that sunlit drive through forested slopes on the first day, she seemed so placid, so transparent. The breeze was gentle, and only the steamiest wisp of threat curled above the distant caldera. But then I broke through the tree line, and suddenly she rose vast and god-like.

Is the mountain you can name the real mountain?

I had come with a group of scientists and writers to camp for four days in July on a ridge that seemed only one giant step below the caldera, the blast zone open to our gaze. We came to the mountain to seek what lessons she might have to teach, or rather what we were capable of learning from the stories we shared about her. Over the course of days and nights, some of us would find that, while our focus was on the mountain, what we glimpsed was closer and even more intimate—ourselves, caught by surprise as we walked and dreamt on that visibly transformed bedrock of change some call catastrophe.

Like many, I often attempt to recognize where I am by comparison to other places I've been. The scrambled openness of the mountaintop reminded me of what I love about the high desert. But the scientists complicated this attempt on my part

to comfort myself with the familiar. They led us on hikes and
bid us to look, and really listen, and discover. Their intention,
I think, was to provoke wonder, and a liberating uncertainty.
They had been humbled, challenged, and finally exhilarated to
find so many of their predictions about the ways that life would
re-inhabit the mountain after the 1980 eruption simply, or
complexly, wrong. The mountain gave them a chance to learn,
re-think, and re-imagine. Could fish survive, after all, in creeks
completely buried by ash ("I felt something moving along the
creekbed, under my boots …")? To witness landscapes and biotic
communities in process, hybrid and adaptive in ways that defy
accepted categories and expectations!

So what you see is not all you get. Like the scientists and their
initial assumptions, my first impression of the mountain was off
the mark. The mountain is never transparent. The unseen—what
is hidden to immediate human perception because of size grand
or small, processes intricate and layered, or sheer time scale—
shapes the air I breathe, the ground I hike, the communities of
plants and creatures, the sounds and sights and very smells of
this mountain. To finally understand this in my mortal bones on
the slopes of this volcano was for me to learn it about all places,
everywhere on earth (welcome home).

Is the mountain you can name the real mountain?

On the first evening in camp most of us gathered to watch the
setting sun turn gigantic billows of dust and vapor around the
caldera into an electric shimmering of pink, red, and then purple.
Maybe, we conceded, it was worth courting disaster, tempting
fate, to spend days and nights so close to the mouth of a volcano.
Somewhere between the awed silences and the occasional skitter
of applause, someone asked: do you think of the mountain as
masculine or feminine, or both, or neither? Female, or both,
came pretty consistently from the writers. Neither, equally as
consistent from the scientists (though there were exceptions, in
both groups). Then a thoughtful pause, an invisible scratching
of heads. Do I have to think about this now? We watched the

caldera darken, the first stars appear. But the question stayed with me. If how we name something not only reflects but also powerfully crafts our relationship with it, how do we address the mountain?

There are descriptive scientific terms I could use, but I am not a geologist or biologist, and this is not a sensibility I regularly inhabit (though I learn a lot from forays into those perspectives). On the other hand, thinking of Mount St. Helens as "her" is a human convention of long standing. Many of the names from the indigenous bands and tribes of this region—the Yakama, Klickitat, Cowlitz, Puyallup and others—gendered the mountain as female (with names such as "Loowit," a name that now graces trails, waterfalls, and schools), while a number of other mountains were considered male. In Pacific Northwestern towns and literary traditions she has for generations been referred to as "the Lady." This is not to say that the relation of indigenous peoples to the mountain is the same as that of the relatively recent invaders and settlers. There are differing understandings among and between all these folks about gender and about "nature." Words carry histories not easily translated or assumed. When "Loowit" becomes "Lady of Fire," what relationships, what understandings are lost in translation? And yet, even if each culture has its own mountain, a language of presence persists.

The mountain you can name is the real mountain, isn't it?

On the trail above Spirit Lake leading to the base of the caldera, we walk in a straggling line, mostly quiet, few conversations. The view is stunning. I remind myself that this what I am looking at: In a handful of moments much of what was here before in the blast zone was blown away or buried. Then communities of plants and animals began to form again. Survivors under the ash—seeds, small mammals, insects, amphibians and reptiles— emerged to a transformed world, a raw, open landscape receptive now to the migration of species that would not have been found here before the eruption. Cataclysm increased biodiversity. We walk through the visible signs of such stories, parables of ash and pumice. The ragged horizon snags the imagination. Along the ridge across from me, I see an entire forest of dead, downed trees, their tops pointing in the same direction. Later that day, I hike through a surviving patch of sturdy old growth just below the shelter of a looming outcrop (who was this a refuge for? who survived here?). It's a landscape material and symbolic, and I am a biological creature who breathes language as surely as air, and these are stories of embodiment, stories that, literally, come with the territory.

Isn't the mountain you can name the real mountain?

It is probably no surprise that the mountain elicits wonder at its marvels, and delight in the intricate and surprising renaissance of life after the eruption. But if you spend enough time here, it can also call forth more troubling emotions. On the ecological scale, the hard truth that death for some means life for others follows a close study of the re-colonized blast zone. Our talk in camp and along the trails ranges from awe to anguish to hope and back again. There is the human scale of what happened here—the deaths of people lost to the eruption—and the deaths of whole ecosystems.

Reminders are everywhere. One death linked to another in an endless chain of loss. What if you'd known Spirit Lake decades before 1980, and you saw your calling, your profession, as a steward of that lake, to nurture the conditions that allowed fish to thrive there? In Spirit Lake you saw qualities that part of you, as a scientist, might disavow as all-too-human projections—vitality, beauty, and the renewal of hope, its seeming permanence in your life promised year after year. After the eruption, the lake was a roiling, thick gray miasma, a medium only for acid-tolerant microbes and parasites, awash with the scorched remnants of what had been a forest. As a scientist, the transformation poses questions for research and learning, and you proceed. Years later, your tears find you, catch you unaware.

Is the mountain you can name the real mountain?

I sit on a stony mound on the edge of camp, my back to the caldera. One story of this mountain for humans, then, at least for some of us, is about mortality and suffering, about impermanence. It is tempting for me to embrace the story of the eruption and its aftermath as one of cataclysm and recovery. And even generalize this to a moral about the irrepressible persistence of life, and by extension find a parable for human hope and ultimate triumph in the face of cataclysm. But I find myself beginning to resist the urge to leap without pause to this comforting conclusion, though I acknowledge its power. There are just more stories to consider. After all, who or what can be said to triumph, even temporarily, in the unfolding of events after the eruption? From where I sit, I see a vivid wash of fireweed just below me, near Ursula's tent. A glory of blooms from broken ground. A wildflower that thrives on disturbance.

To Mount St. Helens

John Daniel

You were the perfect one,
the saint of symmetry.
We glanced at your benign
bright face, and you shined back
your blessing, you smiled
peacefully upon us.
We didn't much believe
Your smoke and stir, we thought
your restiveness would pass—
and then you shuddered hard
and blasted yourself across
four states, engulfed a lake,
gorged rivers with gray mud,
flattened entire forests
and whatever lives they held
in your searing smother.
Your evenness and grace
exploded twelve miles high,
then showered down as grit
on our trim lawns and gardens—
and there you slouch, smudged
and gaping, spewing smoke,
resting in your rubble.
You did it, Mount St. Helens.
As all of us looked on
you stormed in solitude,
you shrugged and shook aside
what we called beautiful
as if none of us were here,

no animals, no trees,
no life at all outside
your ancient fiery joy—
I admired you, mountain,
but I never loved you until now.

Part III

A Gardener Goes to the Volcano

Charles Goodrich

We are walking a trail a few miles northeast of the crater. Though it is late July, here at six thousand feet it is spring, and thousands of wildflowers are blooming. Lupine and penstemon poke up through the foliage of elderberry and hardhack. A steep, spring-watered scree slope is crowded with blossoms—asters and saxifrage, lupine and meadow rue, yarrow and cow parsnip—all so artfully intermingling that my synapses spark. Clearly I am coded to answer to such patterns in the world. Flowers set my blood to humming.

I am an incorrigible gardener. I can't keep my hands off the earth, and if I must keep my hands off, I rearrange and compose it in my mind. I would love to be able to create in my back yard a flower bed as riotously harmonious as this wild one, but it's not possible. An alpine grotto full of spring wildflowers is beyond composition. Such wild spontaneity puts the gardener in his place, aware of his limits. I take a few photographs, make a small bow, and saunter on.

A hundred yards up the trail, I come around a shoulder of the ridge and the world opens onto a staggering panorama. Ahead looms Mount St. Helens, its crater a ragged maw belching steam. A vast plain of pumice slopes away from the crater, the aftermath of the 1980 eruption's massive landsides and pyroclastic flows. All around the distant horizon stand crenellated ridges of seared rock and barren crags, an immense and seemingly empty landscape. Touched by vertigo, I put my hand out to the rock beside me. This is no garden. This is the raw and reckless face of the wild, testimony to immense destruction, the obliteration of landscapes and lives. The prospect rattles me. What is a gardener to make of an active volcano?

That little grotto back down the trail holds some clues. When Mount St. Helens erupted and the northern face of the mountain fell away, the avalanche buried about twenty-three square miles of surrounding forest under hundreds of feet of mud, ash, and debris. The blast leveled another one hundred twenty-five miles of forest, and blanketed the ground in varying depths of ash. And yet, to the astonishment of ecologists monitoring the biological response to these disturbances, within days insects re-appeared, plants germinated, new communities sprang back from such places as the grotto. Shielded from the blast by the flank of the ridge, protected from a deathly ashfall presumably by favorable winds, the grotto is what ecologists call a refugium, a place that remained habitable when the surrounding area was devastated. Surviving plants in refugia such as this were a source of seeds that helped re-colonize disturbed areas. Insects, arthropods, perhaps even small mammals that survived here would have subsequently migrated outward to jumpstart the next ecological stirring of the landscape. Now, twenty-five years later, out on the pumice plain, a vast area where no plants survived the 1980 cataclysm, fields of lupine and other wildflowers are in bloom. Sitka willows and red alder are prospering wherever there's enough water. Nature, unfazed by the eruption, is moving right along.

&- &- &-

Catastrophes always have descendants. My home garden is a hundred and some miles south of Mount St. Helens in the Willamette Valley. The soil there—a beautiful, silty-clay loam, very fertile, and at least thirty feet deep—was deposited by a series of catastrophic floods that occurred between twelve and twenty thousand years ago. Toward the end of the last ice age, immense dams of ice impounded an inland sea, ancient Lake Missoula. As the climate warmed and the ice began to recede, the ice dams repeatedly broke, unleashing floods that inundated lands hundreds of miles away, a series of cataclysms of almost unimaginable power. We know this today because there are boulders the size of Volkswagens that were rafted in icebergs all the way from the Rocky Mountains to be left stranded high on ridges around the Willamette Valley's margins. The floodwaters swirled four hundred feet deep where my house now stands.

If there were humans living there at that time, they would have all perished. Most of the animals large and small surely did. Yet that catastrophe left the parent soil I garden with. That stupendous flood made the Willamette Valley a place of natural abundance, where the native Kalapuya people prospered for centuries, harvesting camas, acorns, tarweed, and other plants, hunting deer and other game animals, and managing the landscape with fire to encourage the growth of food plants and browse for animals, a durable kind of landscape-scale gardening.

That natural abundance drew the wagon trains west in the nineteenth century. Since then, industrial agriculture and urbanization have transformed the valley, changing the landscape as profoundly as volcanism, killing off native plant communities and the animals that depend on them, altering the course of rivers, poisoning aquifers, even driving the farmers themselves from the land.

As a gardener, I, too, am a bringer of catastrophe: every time I spade up a bed, I wreak havoc on the community of organisms in the soil. I clear-cut my corn patch, pull up my beans. I alter the soil with ashes and lime. Though I garden organically, and I don't begrudge a portion of the produce for the birds and the slugs, I cause my share of death and disruption.

It would seem that there is plenty of volcano-like destruction in the garden. But is there anything garden-like on the volcano? The word *garden* derives from European roots that signify *enclosure*; thus a garden is often a place set apart from its surroundings, delimited or enclosed. The little grotto of wildflowers has that quality; surrounded by a rocky outcrop to one side and a bank of shrub-alders on the other, it is a lovely, human-scale place. But the square miles of blown-down forest, the ragged debris heaps of the pumice plain, the crater with its bulging magmatic dome—these seem to be ruled by chaos, by nature uncontained.

And yet, there are walls around all this chaos too. The enclosure surrounding this place is a legal one, an administrative boundary, defining the public commons where certain rules and values apply. I saw the dividing line out past Meta Lake yesterday, where the boundary between the Mount St. Helens National Volcanic Monument and the adjacent National Forest lands is clearly drawn in vegetation. After the 1980 blast, timber companies raced to salvage downed timber from many thousands of acres of private and National Forest lands. But ecologists, environmentalists, and others persuaded Congress to declare much of the land around the crater and extending out across the blasted forest a National Monument, where the land would be allowed to renew itself without human intervention. Salvage logging and industrial forestry were consigned to the lands outside of the Monument boundary.

You can't miss the sharp dividing line: it's drawn in green trees and it climbs the ridge straight as the bottom line on an accountant's ledger, with absolutely no regard for topography. On one side, the replanted fir and hemlock trees are growing thick, even, and strong. On the other side, the naturally revegetated lands are greening up more slowly. The gardener in me understands that, for growing trees, for maximizing a crop, the timber companies and the land itself have done wonders. Here, at the outer edge of the blast area, the ash deposits are thick enough to suppress competing vegetation, but thin enough that the tree seedlings could be planted into the pre-eruption soil. These trees are thriving in soils made rich by tephra-falls.

Across that line, within the Monument, where the land is revegetating naturally, the trees look less vigorous and there are more competing shrub species. But something more interesting is also growing there: a trove of fresh insights for ecologists. The varieties of landscapes inside the Monument represent the entire gradient of volcanic disturbance. On the most heavily impacted areas such as the pumice plain, the former landscape was obliterated, leaving thick new sterile deposits. In other areas, trees were knocked flat and varying amounts of ash and pumice buried the ground. Farther away from the blast, trees were killed but left standing; and farther yet, ash fell, but the trees survived. This array of variously impacted landscapes is a living laboratory, where scientists, and interested amateurs like me, can see how natural processes repopulate altered landscapes in myriad different ways. If the eruption was a catastrophe, it was also a gift. Watching and monitoring how these places are renewing themselves, researchers have been awed and humbled by the biological responses, the resilience of the landscape, the rapidity with which plants and animals have colonized even the most devastated areas. The land knows what to make of cataclysms.

ɞ ɞ ɞ

A curious troupe of scientists and writers, we've been camped for three days on a ridge a few miles east of the crater. It is by no means a regulation campground—just a flat stretch of bulldozed pumice beside the gravel road—but we've made it comfortable. The cooking crew has a truck and kitchen trailer parked to one side. There's a big white dining canopy with tables and chairs enough for all twenty of us to crowd inside when it rains. Our nylon tents are bright dashes of crisp architecture among the surrounding scrub. Somebody has hung a string of prayer flags over the path to the porta-pots. We have made a temporary refuge for ourselves in this harsh, hot place.

In our professional lives, we usually adhere to the limits of our respective disciplines—whether geomorphology or speculative fiction. But here on the mountain we are all exploring the in-between possibilities, the places where fact and metaphor tangle together, where data and story are in dialogue. If we had to share a common label, the only capacious enough word I can think of would be "naturalists." We are a bunch of naturalists, trying to find the connections between butterflies and administrative boundaries, between pyroclastic flows and outbursts of lupines. If we can parse the grammar of the landscape, maybe we'll glimpse the bigger story: What can an active volcano tell us about how to live?

If the refugia on Mount St. Helens are places where old ways persist amidst rapid change, then our backyard gardens must be refugia, too. Our gardens harbor food plants that industrial farmers no longer grow. Our rich garden soils support big populations of arthropods, insects, earthworms, and microorganisms. These in turn become nourishment for reptiles, rodents, and birds. My garden abounds in garter snakes.

But more importantly, for me at least, gardening itself is an act of refuge. Attending to plants, regarding the weather, interacting closely with wild animals (and I'm thinking more of beetles, chickadees, and gophers than large game animals), working the soil with hand tools and bare hands: these are millennia-old human experiences that seem to be, at least in some over-developed countries, at risk. Who could have imagined such a sea change in the texture of daily experience? Our gardens are one of the places we can keep up both the seed pool and our own animal resilience, and maybe cultivate a wry sense of perspective along the way.

Earthquakes, tsunamis, and volcanic eruptions; forest fires and range fires; floods, mudslides, and droughts—catastrophe happens. Maybe volcano watching will make us better gardeners, help us tend the refugia that our homes, towns, and cities actually are. And maybe gardening can help us be more aware of the surge and roar of land.

Evolutionary Impacts of a Blasted Landscape

Jerry F. Franklin

I have been learning and evolving with the post-eruption Mount St. Helens landscape for over twenty-five years—about half of my professional life. This collaborative journey has moved me to continuously alter my views of ecological disturbances and the concept of "recovery"—and the evolution of both landscape and mind continue! Major intellectual change began with the shock of my first visit to the blast zone following the May 1980 eruption. I thought that I had some pretty good ideas about how the post-eruption landscape would evolve, and most of my preconceptions proved dead wrong. For starters, my initial notion was that the post-eruption Mount St. Helens landscape would be a "moonscape"—and I was not alone in that view. But that notion was instantly dispelled as I stepped out of the helicopter on my first landing within the blast zone: just a few days after the eruption, here were hundreds of plants pushing their way up through the mantle of fresh tephra.

Surviving organisms were stunning in their diversity and abundance, and the mechanisms by which they survived. Some persisted as intact individuals living below ground, encased within late-spring snowbanks, and buried in lake and stream sediment. Others survived as segments of rhizomes (root-like horizontal underground stems) transported along with the massive landslide that initiated the eruption. Yet others survived as stems that were able to sprout new leaves and roots after abrasion and even transportation by mudflows. These mudflows also floated nurse logs—downed and decaying tree trunks with young tree seedlings growing on them—and re-deposited them on the floor of a floodplain forest. Millions of plants survived as rootstocks and rhizomes and yet others survived on root wads of uprooted trees in the expansive blast zone.

Wood—snags, entire tree boles, and other smaller woody debris—was everywhere in the blast zone, beginning to fulfill its long-term and diverse functions. These woody structures created habitat for animals, fungi, and microbes, serving as sediment traps, energy and nutrient sources, and protective cover for tree seedlings, small fish, and mammals hiding from predators.

One of the great delights of my frequent early visits to Mount St. Helens was continually discovering further mechanisms by which living nature had survived the eruption. Many were logical in retrospect (if not in prospect!) while many others were counterintuitive. Survival often involved stochastic circumstances—the result of chance events. The multiplicity of disturbances, both individual and combined, resulted in an immense diversity of post-eruptive conditions, ranging from minimally impacted to completely obliterated. Most places within the blast zone actually were affected by two or three different types of disturbances. Some impacts extended far beyond the immediate vicinity of the mountain, particularly tephra depositions, which fell on forests, farmlands, and cities far to the east.

Biological Legacies

The concept of "biological legacies" emerged from this very diverse collection of surviving biota and masses of dead wood. Living legacies from the pre-eruption landscape survived to quickly populate and jump-start recovery of forests, meadows, lakes, and streams. Logs and snags provided habitat for both surviving and colonizing organisms. Great insight was not necessary—ecologists investigating the blast zone had their noses rubbed daily in the evidence of legacies and their importance.

Mount St. Helens catalyzed the concept of biological legacies as well as many other important additions and modifications to our basic understanding of ecosystem responses to disturbance—

"secondary succession" in ecological lingo. Why should so much fundamental learning have occurred since the lessons are so obvious in retrospect? Perhaps it was the magnitude of the event, which led many of us to that early and incorrect perception of a moonscape. Perhaps because many previous ecological studies of secondary succession focused on re-establishment of forests in abandoned agricultural fields—sites with limited legacies of organisms and wood. Handy as these old fields were to early centers of ecological science, they were not representative of conditions and processes following natural disturbances.

Whatever the explanation, the importance of biological legacies now is evident to disturbance ecologists everywhere, whether their focus is fundamental or applied. Indeed, one might propose that the most important factors influencing post-disturbance recovery processes are the types and levels of biological legacies that are present—not the type, intensity, size, or any other attribute of the disturbance, as is often proposed. At least, legacies are among the most important predictors of the rate and direction of post-disturbance ecological development.

The concept of biological legacies has similarly impacted applied ecology—specifically forest practices. The dominant tree-harvest technique of clear-cutting obviously produces conditions that have little similarity to natural disturbances such as fire, wind, and even volcanic eruption. Clear-cutting leaves little in the way of biological legacies. Natural disturbances with their structural legacies are providing improved models for forest practices where maintenance of biological diversity and natural ecosystem functions are primary or collateral goals of forest management, such as on our federal timberlands. The concept of variable retention harvesting—a silvicultural system in which varying types, amounts, and patterns of living trees, snags, and logs are left to lifeboat organisms and structurally enrich the regenerating forest—emerged from research at Mount St. Helens.

Spatial Patterns of Ecological Responses

Mount St. Helens is providing us with other important big-picture perspectives on large disturbances, such as patterns of recolonization. The Mount St. Helens landscape we see today is expansive and complex, with high contrasts. There are biological hotspots composed of lush patches of vegetation occupied by small mammals, birds, and other creatures. There are also sparsely vegetated coldspots where erosional processes have retarded or repeatedly reset ecological development.

Ecological recovery in the Mount St. Helens blast zone began with hundreds of thousands of hotspots composed of surviving organisms. Some of these hotspots were as small as individual plants while others were large patches of virtually intact communities, such as those surviving within or under late-lying snowbanks. "Metastasizing" is a term that I have used to characterize recovery processes within the blast zone; it conveys the sense of multiple centers of colonization (or, in other contexts, "infection") that grow, spread, and eventually converge. This pattern of colonization contrasts sharply with the "wave-front" model often used in hypothesizing about recovery patterns in large, intensely disturbed areas. The wave-front model proposes a gradual reinvasion of the disturbed area from its margins inward.

Some of the hotspots of recovery at Mount St. Helens were also particularly hospitable environmental patches, such as wetlands on the debris avalanche. These were of great importance in both plant and amphibian recolonization.

Ecological Role of Large Disturbed Areas

Mount St. Helens has been and most profoundly remains a landscape that instructs us about the ecological roles that are played by large, slowly reforesting disturbed areas within an otherwise forested region. Indeed, my experiences at Mount St. Helens have moved me to re-examine my whole notion about what is meant by "recovery" within a forested landscape—but more about that in a moment.

Currently one of the most significant ecological attributes of the Mount St. Helens blast zone is its biological diversity. There are large and diverse populations of major animal groups, such as songbirds, amphibians, and medium-sized predators, such as coyotes and bobcats. The wide variety of structural conditions and food sources support a rich avifauna, which includes a large variety of species that are characteristic of the western Cascade Range as well as several that are quite unexpected, such as the western meadowlark. Amphibian diversity is high—fifteen species out of a possible eighteen are present. As important, some amphibian species, such as the western toad, are prolific reproducers in the Mount St. Helens landscape. Richness and abundance of many small and middle-sized mammals are also high.

The Mount St. Helens blast zone is unquestionably a regional hotspot of biological diversity in terms of species diversity and population densities. Critical factors in creating and sustaining this animal diversity are (1) the presence of the full array of biological legacies including live trees, snags, and logs, and (2) compositionally and structurally diverse early-successional communities (i.e., the limited occurrence of dense, closed coniferous forest cover). Conditions in this early-successional community contrast greatly with those in disturbed areas that have been salvaged (legacies removed) and replanted with dense stands of conifers (plantations).

Another way Mount St. Helens' blast zone contrasts with the typical regional landscape is that the blast zone has extensive areas dominated by hardwood trees and shrubs as opposed to conifers. Red alder and black cottonwood are conspicuous, the alder by its numbers and the cottonwood by its rapid growth rate and height. Sitka alder is an aggressive shrubby species that has profited dramatically from the eruption, surviving on essentially all previously occupied habitat and colonizing much additional territory. A diversity of conifer species has seeded in at low densities. However, dense stands of conifers are found only where they were planted following the eruption or where advance regeneration survived within snowbanks.

In addition to the diversity of species, life forms, and communities in this early-successional landscape a diversity of important ecological functions is also underway. One especially important process is the biological fixation of nitrogen by microbes associated with some of the dominant plants in the landscape, including legumes, such as lupines, and several non-leguminous species, such as the alders.

I expect that these ecologically diverse conditions, including large areas that are unoccupied by closed forests, will continue to dominate the unsalvaged, unplanted portions of the Mount St. Helens blast zone for many future decades. The closed-canopy coniferous forest so characteristic of this region is going to be a long time in coming! Meanwhile, the gradually evolving landscape will continue to serve as a marvelous source for new ecological understanding.

The biological richness of the Mount St. Helens landscape is relevant to current debates about appropriate activities following major wildfires and other disturbances. Timber salvage and aggressive reforestation have been accepted policy and are often aggressively pursued. As a consequence, naturally disturbed, early-successional habitat, which has been neither salvaged or planted, is probably the scarcest of the natural forestland states in the productive, low-elevation regions of the Pacific Northwest, rarer than even old-growth forest.

Is "Recovery" the Appropriate Perspective?

In 2005 I spent many days viewing and photographing conditions at Mount St. Helens after twenty-five years of ecological response to the 1980 eruptions. I began to wonder why I had been using the term "recovery" in relation to this landscape, since implicit in the word is the notion of a return to some pre-existing condition.

Here was a landscape of great complexity and richness, a landscape with extraordinary levels of biological diversity. In this region characterized by closed forests and clear-cuts, the altered landscape of Mount St. Helens was truly a hotspot for many life forms, species, and important ecological processes. Why was I thinking about the blast zone in terms of its recovery to a dense coniferous forest dominance that had existed prior to the eruption (and, of course, prior to the clear-cutting of extensive portions of the landscape)? Was I really anxious for the Mount St. Helens blast zone to recover to closed-canopy coniferous forest? If the management objective for the area was wood production, then rapid recovery to coniferous forest dominance would be appropriate, but that was not the objective within the national volcanic monument.

The blast zone is making extraordinary contributions to regional biological diversity in its current state of diverse early-successional conditions. Given societal agreement on management objectives, why would anyone want to artificially truncate this state? Why would we want to hurry this landscape along to a state of conifer dominance? The mountain seems to teach that significant current ecological value is to be found in the conditions, organisms, and processes characterizing this diverse successional landscape. "Recovery" is probably not the best word to use.

Closing Thoughts

My first encounter with the Mount St. Helens country came when I was a child, on family camping trips from our home in the small industrial town of Camus, Washington, a few tens of miles south along the Columbia River. I went back to that country as a Ph.D. student at Washington State University, studying the forests of the southern Washington Cascades. The 1980 eruption of Mount St. Helens brought me back again to see what new lessons the mountain had to offer. And what lessons they are! Mount St. Helens has provided one of the largest and most complex natural disturbance events accessible for intense study and reflection in our time. Paradigm-busting science has emerged and, hopefully, some paradigm-busting policy as well!

This Mount St. Helens landscape is full of surprising details and idiosyncratic species as well as broad lessons regarding the physical and biological processes associated with destruction and stabilization.

Mount St. Helens is not about "recovery" to some future forested state. It is about its natural evolution, its rich array of organisms and processes, and its contributions to our ecological understanding. Mount St. Helens can teach us to think better about catastrophic events. It can also help us construct natural resource policies based on logic and on "good" science.

I am blessed to have spent half a century living, studying, playing, and reflecting in the shadow of Mount St. Helens. Little did I know what the mountain would do during my lifetime, or how profoundly those events would affect my thinking. I know I have learned a great deal, but I am sure that the mountain and its landscape will continue to provide lessons for me for the rest of my life!

Mountains and Mosses

Nalini M. Nadkarni

Trees and mountains are symbols of stability and endurance. Just as mountain peaks persist over evolutionary time, so do trees outlast human lifetimes. The word "tree" comes from the Sanskrit root word *deru*, which means to be firm or solid. The words endure, shelter, truce, and true are also derived from *deru*. Although they exemplify constancy, both mountains and trees are subject to disturbances that can wreak dramatic changes in their form and in the complement of organisms with which they are associated. A volcanic eruption is a dynamic force that has tremendous effects on the trees that populate the mountain's flanks, as can be seen in the legions of fallen trunks and broken crowns still visible twenty-five years after the explosion of Mount St. Helens.

Trees have always held my interest and my trust. As a child, I climbed the sugar maple (*Acer saccharum*) trees in the front yard of my family's home, finding the best routes up, reading books in branchnooks, and watching squirrels jump from limb to limb. The trees' strong branches provided a refuge from the sometimes chaotic world of my large and culturally mixed family. As a graduate student in the 1980s, I studied forest ecology and learned how to use mountain-climbing equipment to get access to the canopy, the "last biological frontier." For three decades, I have carried out treetop research in tropical rainforests and in the Pacific Northwest. I focus on epiphytes, the plants that grow on other plants (*epi* means upon; *phyte* means plant).

Although canopy plants reach their greatest diversity in tropical rainforests, tree crowns in the Pacific Northwest support hundreds of species of epiphytes—mainly mosses and lichens. As these plants die and decompose on branch surfaces, they create a highly organic arboreal soil, which knits together the living plants and dead organic matter into a rug-like "moss mat" that covers branch and trunk surfaces of the large, old trees. When I climb into a single bigleaf maple (*Acer macrophyllum*) tree in old-growth forests of this region, I can find as many as eighty species of mosses and lichens.

The peculiar anatomy and physiology of epiphytes allows them to play important ecological roles in our forests. Because epiphytes have no true roots, they take up water and nutrients through their foliage, which is only one cell layer thick. Rainfall provides water and necessary mineral elements for these plants. Each drop of rain is composed of a tiny central nucleus of dust—which contains nutrients such as nitrogen and calcium—around which water vapor coalesces. When rain passes over the surface of a moss or lichen, the plant absorbs and retains the rain's nutrients. When the moss dies and falls to the ground to decompose, its nutrients enter the mineral cycles of the forest. Thus, these tiny, canopy-dwelling plants serve collectively as a giant sponge to intercept nutrients from the atmosphere, which ultimately circulate throughout the forest landscape. Canopy moss mats also provide a critical substrate for insects and nesting materials, which are used by arboreal animals such as marbled murrelets (*Brachyramphus marmoratus*) and northern flying squirrels (*Glaucomys sabrinus*).

Epiphytes have a remarkable ability to survive and reproduce in their exposed canopy environments, where they experience extremes of relative humidity and high levels of sunlight and wind. However, epiphytes are fragile in the face of physical disturbances. I know from watching arboreal primates and climbing trees myself that it is very easy to kick off chunks of moss mats, exposing patches of bark. Sometimes, the sheer weight of a saturated mat will create an "epi-slide," in which the whole mat slides off, exposing the entire naked branch. In addition, the increasing practice of harvesting epiphytic moss for the growing horticulture trade is putting greater pressure on wild populations of epiphytes in the Pacific Northwest. Epiphytes are also sensitive to changes in their normal environmental conditions. Experimental evidence shows that predicted changes in global climate patterns will negatively affect these canopy-dwelling plants. If epiphytes were to decline or disappear because of physical disturbances or environmental changes, the capacity of the forest to maintain a balanced nutrient cycle and to provide resources to arboreal animals might also decline.

Because these small and seemingly insignificant plants play important ecological roles, I was curious to know about their ability to regenerate if they are removed or disturbed. In the 1980s, my students and I conducted experiments in Pacific Northwest forests to measure the recolonization of mosses by clearing branches of their mosses. At regular intervals, we returned to our stripped patches and documented the plants that appeared. Because the existing mosses grow so luxuriantly in these habitats, we had anticipated that the moss would grow back and fill up the blank spaces within months. Surprisingly, it took over a decade for the first epiphytes to come back at all. First, the paper-like crustose lichens appeared, followed by a slimy coating of green algae that colonized the bare bark on the underside of the branch. This was followed by foliose—or leaf—lichens. After nearly twenty years we finally found the species of mosses that had occupied the original branch space. Apparently, these old-growth mosses require the texture and moisture-holding capacity provided by the early colonizers.

After these studies, I wanted to understand the dynamics of moss substrate, to understand the movement and longevity of the branches on which epiphytes perch. To do so, I shifted my focus from the whole forest and whole trees to a much smaller spatial scale. Studying the forest from the treetops provides many different perspectives. Most ground-bound humans tend to look at trees from the standpoint of a whole single tree, rooted permanently in the ground. Those who study mountains tend to view the forest at the level of the entire landscape. But canopy researchers see trees in a wide range of spatial scales. When I perch on the uppermost branch of an emergent tree and look out across the outer envelope of the forest, I get the grand view, the perspective of a raptor soaring over the broccoli-shaped crowns of trees below. When I take data on the length that a frond of moss has grown in a month, I work at the spatial scale of hundredths of an inch. To study the canopy at the spatial scale appropriate to moss recolonization, I needed to document dynamics at the scale of a single branch.

To do this, I dipped the tip of a paintbrush in green paint and tied it to the tip of a branch. I sat in a spot from which I could comfortably hold up a piece of white paper at exactly where the branch tip held the loaded paintbrush. I set my watch for two minutes. A gentle breeze moved the twig to and fro, and as it brushed against the paper, I was delighted to see the brush strokes marking the page. Up and down, back and forth, the twig moved in the wind and the paint and paper recorded its journey. After two minutes, the combination of tree and wind and brush created an image.

To estimate the total number of twigs on the tree, I counted the number of twigs on that branchlet, the number of branchlets on a branch, and the number of branch systems on the whole tree. I then measured and summed up the distance of all of the lines that had been produced by that twig in two minutes. I extrapolated the total distance that the whole tree's twigs moved based on the total distance and the total number of twigs. I was amazed to learn that the collective distance that the twigs of this one tree moved in one year was 286,400 miles, or more than ten times around the world.

This exercise made me aware of the dynamics of trees from a different perspective. Normally, we think of trees as being rooted in the ground, of staying in one place, of having the qualities of *deru*. This awareness reminded me of a gripping poem, written by a Bengali poet, Vijaya Mukhopadhyay, that brings a vivid sense of urgency to the reader using the improbable desire of a rooted tree wanting to move as a metaphor for the struggle to accomplish a dream against all odds.

> *Wanting to Move*
> Continually, a bell rings in my heart.
> I was supposed to go somewhere, to some other place,
> Tense from the long wait
> Where do you go, will you take me
> "With you, on your horses, down the river, with the flames of your
>   torches?"
>
> They burst out laughing.
> "A tree wanting to move from place to place?"
> Startled, I look at myself—
> A tree, wanting to move from place to place, a tree
> Wanting to move? Am I then—
> Born here, to die here
> Even die here?
> Who rings the bell, then, inside my heart?
> Who tells me to go, inside my heart?
> Who agitates me, continually, inside my heart?

I think of this poem when I am involved in the improbable dream of moving society towards protecting trees from the human activities that are causing loss of diversity and imbalances in forest functions. An increasing part of my professional life has been to infuse in others the sense of importance, interest, and wonder that I see in trees and their canopy associates. I especially try to connect with audiences who traditionally do not seek out information on nature or science—urban youth, prisoners, and disabled people. By raising awareness about the importance of trees and other parts of the natural world, I am in a small way paying back the trees for their having provided me a childhood refuge, providing me with a rich source of intellectual stimulation, and maintaining the health of ecosystems around us.

One way to facilitate communication, and to open up new ways of knowing and communicating with these audiences, is for scientists to interact with artists, creative writers, and humanists. Thus, it was with great anticipation that I joined the Mount St. Helens foray in the summer of 2005 to explore the theme of destruction and recovery with other ecologists, poets, and philosophers. I anticipated that I would gain both insights into the ecological dynamics of recovery, and access to other ways of thinking and writing about the phenomena.

For the first two days, activities unfolded as I had expected. Our campsite was located within the blast zone, surrounded by trees that were killed and fell instantly when exposed to the eruption. Over the ensuing twenty-five years, little decomposition of the fallen trunks has taken place, and they lie as they did a quarter of a century ago. I listened as the ecologists reconfirmed my understanding that the eruption of this mountain is an ongoing part of the natural disturbance regime, and that trees and their associates have encountered disturbances multiple times over their evolutionary history. I took in the fact that these species are resilient and have endured many such eruptions over the millennia. I compared the patterns of successional events documented for the vegetation on the mountain to the procession of moss species that I had observed on my cleared branches, and I played with the idea of parallel patterns between mountain and tree: the existence of specialized colonizer species, "hot spots" of recolonization, and facilitation of the microenvironment for later successional species.

It was a pleasure and a comfort to the scientific parts of my brain to work out these ecological puzzles. But after a few days of seeing and stepping over and sleeping next to the trunks of so many dead trees, I felt an unexpected pool of deep sadness in my chest. I did not wish to admit to this, since scientists are supposed to understand the world with the head, not the heart. During our campfire discussion that evening, as darkness settled upon our group, individuals in turn spoke of their experiences and emotions relating to the destruction of trees, starting first with natural forces, such as the volcano, but then moving towards those instigated by humans. The poets used language so powerfully. They gathered and spoke their phrases carefully, taking the time they needed to shape a metaphor that would bring sharp clarity to the images they needed to evoke. As I listened, that pool of sadness expanded, like the inexorable bulge of the volcano, until I could no longer contain it. A deep grief for those supine trees all around us poured from me into the night. I felt embarrassed. There is an unspoken taboo for scientists to show emotions about a phenomenon as natural as a volcanic eruption causing trees to fall. But all of the participants treated me with compassion. Perhaps they had felt the same sadness and were glad to have it voiced. I remained in a state of bewilderment for the rest of the night and the following day, perplexed that my intellectual understanding could not override the emotions of loss.

The next day, our group visited an intact forest adjacent to the blast zone. I looked up to the canopy. A companion pointed out an amazing sight: a spider had built a web high in the treetops, between two branches that swayed in different directions. Fragile, beautiful, strong; it was a gift to see this tiny bit of life's complexity weaving her achingly delicate filigree just fifty paces from the cemetery of fallen trees that had been blasted by the mountain's force.

After our foray was over, I reflected on the interwoven facts and feelings that came from examining destruction and recovery of the mountain. I recognized that the emotional connections forged by my physical intimacy to the dead trees, coupled with the evocative voices of the poets and the scientific background we were given, were strong forces in wakening my awareness of how trees and I are linked. Understanding and successfully communicating the importance of the links between nature and humans may lie in merging the complementary forces of science and poetry.

Everlasting Wilderness

Christine Colasurdo

As a native of Portland, Christine Colasurdo grew up camping and hiking at Mount St. Helens. Her family owned a cabin one mile from Spirit Lake and spent time there year-round. In 1979 Colasurdo worked as a waitress and maid at Harmony Falls Lodge, a remote resort on Spirit Lake's east shore that was accessible only by boat or a three-mile trail. A high-school senior, she had planned to return to work at the lodge for the summer of 1980. But it took many years after the May 18, 1980 eruption before she could physically return to Spirit Lake. Not only were roads closed and destroyed, it was difficult for her to confront the changed land. Both her family's cabin and Harmony Falls Lodge had been obliterated. The following chapter is excerpted from her book, Return to Spirit Lake (1997), *which recounts her journey through Mount St. Helens' blast zone to rediscover the land she knew as a child.*

My return to Spirit Lake began the day I happened upon a wildflower so common some call it a weed. Our group of four had set up camp high above Spirit Lake when I noticed it at dusk one late-summer evening. Nighthawks swooped about. A coyote bark drifted up from the east arm of Spirit Lake, 2,000 feet below. We stood, ears clipped by a chill wind, on a 5,000-foot-high ridge as the day came to a close and the sky opened. A summer storm that had drenched the area earlier was clearing off, cloud by cloud. The sharp edges of twisted snags and cracked branches softened in the twilight as the last cumulus in Mount St. Helens' crater slipped west, disclosing the volcano's dome. Spirit Lake's steep basin filled slowly with shadows, but sunlight still caught the crater rim and, in the distance, the snowy summits of Mount Hood, Mount Adams, and Mount Rainier. We were high up on the ridge's spine, at eye level with four of the Cascade Range's major mountains, the only shining things in the wake of the setting sun.

That was when I first glimpsed, after years of shouldering the loss of a vast green landscape, how I might find a path out of my grief—a grief so strange it seemed more like vertigo than mourning. For one thing, the Spirit Lake wilderness bore a strange new name—"blast zone"—to define the area where the volcano's lateral explosion had swept through, blowing trees over and burning them. The words bespoke violence, as though I were returning to a bombed-out house. Worse still, the lake and its surrounding ridges deserved their new name. For 230 square miles the land was so changed its volcanic aftermath had to be catalogued: *scorch zone, blowdown zone, mudflow, pyroclastic flow.* What were those? The first few times I saw Spirit Lake after the eruption, I looked everywhere—at my feet, straight ahead, to the side—trying desperately to get my bearings. Here was once a river. There, a shaded beach. Over there, a grove of old cottonwoods. And on all of the ridges—trees. Everywhere I turned, what should have been lush and cool was desiccated and barren. Low valleys were high; dry land was now water; dark forests were sunbaked plains. *I've been here before,* I murmured each time. But not only had I lost an entire landscape, I myself was lost—a stranger in what should have been familiar land.

But that summer evening, after zigzagging up through the backcountry's blast-flattened forests, I finally found a compass to guide me back to the past. There, at my feet, blooming undisturbed in the rain-patted ash, was a four-foot-wide clump of pearly everlasting, a flower that had once bloomed all around Spirit Lake. Like a ghost returned from the forested past, the tall-stemmed wildflower illuminated its small patch of earth with creamy blossoms flaming with failing sunlight. The narrow, spearlike leaves glowed a soft green. Each stem terminated in a fist of white flowers. Nothing grew within two feet of the clump, which appeared to be about three summers old. I could tell the plant's approximate age because scattered below the upright stems were dead ones—the withered skeletons of the previous summer. And below those were others, fanning out in matted rags across the dark ash.

I might as well have tripped over the doorstep of that bombed-out house. Here was something I could understand. Pearly everlasting was one of the last wildflowers I had seen at Spirit Lake before the eruption. I had sketched it, picked it, dried it. I knew its shape and size, could recall the exact places where it had bloomed—and here it was again. I looked south, east, and north at the sunlit Cascade mountains I had known since childhood, four alpine islands in an ocean of temperate green foothills. Volcanoes. I stood next to the everlasting clump as it shook slightly in the wind, and waited for the last bit of light to abandon the land.

Like many wildflowers at Spirit Lake, pearly everlasting *(Anaphalis margaritacea)* is a perennial herb that rises after each snow melt. Its Latin name, *margaritacea,* means "pearly" and describes the small, beady flowers that are composed of white, papery "involucral bracts" instead of petals. The bracts encircle the tiny yellow florets containing a hundred thread-thin seeds. If picked before they mature, the blossoms—bracts and all—remain intact indefinitely when dried, hence the plant's name. I thought of the everlasting flowers I had dried before the eruption. They had kept their shape and scent for years until I had forgotten about them. Where were those flowers now?

Pink light crept up the first of the four Cascade mountains encircling me. The shortest, youngest, and most violent, for forty thousand years this volcano had pummeled the land where I stood with searing winds, ash, and pumice. Light struck the dark basalt of one of its old lava domes. It was the peak closest to me, a hundred beats of a raven's wing away. Gusts ruffled the lake's surface. Bats joined the nighthawks to feed. I counted the stems of the pearly everlasting beside me: nineteen.

Although pearly everlasting is common in North America and northeast Asia, no one has paid much attention to it. Nineteenth-century naturalists like Thomas Nuttall and David Douglas ignored it. Thoreau considered it the "artificial" flower of September pastures, and the Scandinavian author Neltje Blanchan asked, "Who loves it?" She denigrated the wildflower as "stiff, dry, soulless, quite in keeping with the decorations on the average farmhouse mantelpiece . . . the most uncheering of winter bouquets." At the turn of the century, the wildflower reached its pinnacle of usefulness as the principal flower in funeral wreaths.

But here, at my feet, the illuminated flowers were glowing, cold, swaying in the wind, cupping their seeds in bracts that folded like tiny frozen roses. A plane soared over the lake basin, then disappeared west down the Toutle River. Behind me, the backcountry lakes were jammed with logs, steeped in night. Before me, the peach glow hummed: light was leaving that first mountain.

Native people in the Northwest have also, for the most part, been indifferent to pearly everlasting. Most tribes have neither a name nor use for it. On the Olympic Peninsula, the Quileutes traditionally used the plant in a steam bath for rheumatism, but the Makah forbade their children to play with it because it caused sores. Pearly everlasting can't be eaten like wapato, camas, or wild ginger. It has no berries to rival those of huckleberry, thimbleberry, Oregon grape, or even salal. It lacks the medicinal properties of Pacific yew or cedar. Its blossoms wax sallow next to purple penstemon or orange columbine.

However, over the last three centuries, as the Northwest's woods have been burned, logged, and sliced by roads, pearly everlasting has been useful in one regard: as an erosion-controlling colonizer. Because of its "weedy" properties—vigorous growth, prodigious seeds, and resilience to extreme conditions—pearly everlasting has often been one of the first plants to revegetate a clearcut or burn. Within months of fire or logging, pearly everlasting will sprout in a sunny patch and, along with fireweed, will brighten the spaces between the blackened snags with tall, waving stems loaded with blossoms. By autumn, the two will compete to litter their surroundings with seeds so light they float on the slightest updraft.

Light left the second Cascade mountain—a narrow cone that trembled from time to time with shallow earthquakes. Only fifty miles west of its summit, thousands of people in the Portland metropolitan area were finishing dinner at this moment, washing plates, putting children to bed, thinking of anything but sulfurous fumes rising from one of its warm vents. Pearly everlasting flourished at that mountain, too.

When Mount St. Helens erupted in 1980, it exploded sideways, knocking down thousands of acres of forests. As a result, mountainsides that once held cool, shaded forests were now as sunny and exposed as any clearcut or burn. This seemingly lifeless terrain was inhospitable for many deep-forest species, but for pearly everlasting it was a vast new land upon which the flower could scatter its progeny. Along with fireweed, lupine, thimbleberry, and groundsel, everlasting was sprouting in the blast zone within three months of the May 18 eruption.

I remembered the pearly everlasting flowers near my family's cabin. They had lined the highway to the mountain like beach foam lapping against the conifers. This was a plant that loved sunlight and didn't care how it obtained it. No wonder it was prospering here, atop a windblown ridge.

As a "generalist," pearly everlasting was well equipped to reinhabit Mount St. Helens' harsh terrain. A tough opportunist, the adaptable wildflower wields silver-green leaves whose color deflects the blast zone's intense solar radiation. From stem to leaf tip, the plant is covered in tiny white hairs that trap heat during freezing subalpine nights. Its tenacious roots and rhizomes knit themselves so tightly into the pumice soil, no gust can extract them. But perhaps most importantly, the plant is able to sprout from mere root fragments, and its plentiful feather-light seeds catch the blast zone's winds to colonize vast distances. It is a wildflower that thrives on disaster.

Shadows moved up the third Cascade mountain. Like the others, that volcano had erupted for thousands of years. It, too, could blacken the eastern sky in moments with stinging, suffocating ash. Its northern neighbor, the fourth and tallest, had erupted with massive mudflows into Puget Sound. Pearly everlasting grew on those volcanoes, too.

Five years after the eruption, pearly everlasting was the most common wildflower in the blast zone. The flower swept over the landscape with the same abandon as the eruption itself, clinging to eroded cliffs, plains of loose pumice, and log-jammed hillsides. But while Mount St. Helens' eruption was dramatic, immediate, and televised around the world, everlasting's quiet, seasonal advance transpired with little acclaim. Only scientists noticed that it was improving the harsh habitat for other living things— that it was providing mulch for the volcanic ash, shade and food for insects and rodents, and an anchor for other seeds.

The cold began to cut through layers of wool; the wind howled over rocks. My eyes teared. Below, Spirit Lake's giant log raft—all that remained of the trees surrounding the lake—was breaking up. The raft was created when the volcano erupted sideways, causing a giant wave that washed all the trees into the water. Now, pushed by wind, the massive raft was moving, log by log, to the other end of the lake. It was time to go back to camp. Only a little light remained.

As pearly everlasting reappeared in the blast zone, so too did the mountain's other flowers. As I stood on the ridgetop, I noticed tangles of fireweed five feet high. Beyond them rustled meadows of pasqueflower, paintbrush, and false-hellebore. Shrubby willows and alders were emerging as green spheres on the brown slopes. Huckleberry shrubs proffered tiny blue berries. Young noble and silver firs rose up in evergreen islands, fifteen feet high. Coyotes who had survived after the eruption on little else than insect carcasses now had fragrant wild strawberries to feast upon. The trail we had taken to the ridge was littered with strawberry-studded coyote scat.

I looked up: one star. I rubbed my nose: ice. Then I looked at the volcanoes: nothing. The everlasting clump, too, had gone dark. I bent down and buried my face in its flowers to inhale their beeswax fragrance. The drab pearls in my palms were a tunnel to the inhumed past—when Norway Pass was shady and cool, when the North Fork of the Toutle River sang under its burden of snow; when Spirit Lake, clear of its log raft, reflected at night clouds of stars.

I released the beads and the plant swung back. I was shouldering an old loss like a chunk of wet firewood, but at dusk on the ridge east of Mount Margaret I paused beside a flower some call a weed and rested.

And when coyotes howled around our camp at midnight, I rose from the tent to look at the stars. The lake's logs had disappeared west, disclosing its east arm—a huge, flat path of sparkling obsidian. I gazed up at the sky, then at the same image below: there were the stars, clouds and clouds of them, tiny ice-white flecks in the lake's black waters. The last time I had seen them, the lake was 200 feet lower, and hundreds of trees had crowded its shores. Now it was higher and wider and could accommodate more of the heavens. Thousands of stars floated below, constellations beyond my comprehension. The coyotes' cries drifted for miles across the broken timber. Lost in the galaxies, I took one wide look at the dark land around me. So this was the blast zone.

Science Tribes on Mount St. Helens

James Sedell

I grew up camping in the Cascade Range, fishing the pristine alpine lakes up along the backbone of Oregon's high mountains. I knew the waters of that country as a kid, and, later, as an aquatic ecologist. As the helicopter flew me and several other scientists to the shore of Spirit Lake, I kept reminding myself that the waters of the blasted landscape around the volcano would bear no resemblance to the waters of my childhood. Even so, as I stepped out at the shore of Spirit Lake, I was awestruck. The world had been rocked. All my boyhood recollections of cold, clear alpine lakes and streams in the shadows of tall conifers were blasted away, changed into a landscape of uniform gray. My extensive scientific knowledge of the way these waters once were was simply irrelevant. It was a staggering and disorienting encounter. My first footsteps into that alien landscape began an important journey into scientific and personal discovery.

My science career up to that point had been rooted in ecosystem research, studying fast, cold streams flowing through lush old-growth forests in the Oregon Cascades, landscapes much like those of Mount St. Helens before the eruption. I had worked on the ecological functions of wood in streams and helped develop the scientific rationale for retaining logs and other woody materials in streams. But here on post-eruption Mount St. Helens, square miles of massive old-growth forests had been toppled into lakes and streams. Despite having worked for years in Pacific coast old-growth forests, I had never seen so much wood in streams. What would be the consequences of such large-scale additions of wood into fresh waters? Would Spirit Lake, now a primordial soup choked with logs and void of oxygen, ever have clear water, or harbor fish and wildlife again?

At the same time, the eruption had created entirely *new* ponds and streams that included absolutely no wood, no fish, nor any other vertebrate life. How would these aquatic systems change over the coming years? Strange microbial life forms appeared in thermal seeps and hissing fumaroles, even in spots as inhospitable as the lava dome growing in the crater. What enabled these organisms to survive and prosper in such hostile environments?

No one could begin to answer such questions working alone, but if we could assemble a large group of scientists with experience and training in many different disciplines, we could hope to harvest an enormous wealth of ecological insights. So, in the summer of 1980, just three months after the eruption, I helped convene what we called a "field pulse," gathering nearly two hundred scientists from all over the country on Mount St. Helens. With funding from the Forest Service and National Science Foundation, we rented a camp northeast of the volcano, leased a fleet of vans, and chartered three Jet Ranger helicopters for access to the crater and other areas rendered inaccessible by the eruption. We encouraged strong links among terrestrial, aquatic, and geological scientists and brought in new players to carry out studies on topics that seemed ripe, but neglected. Each day for two weeks we would go to the field in small teams and do our own work, then return to camp and share stories, insights, questions in the evening.

I had been primed for this personal encounter with Mount St. Helens a decade earlier, when I first encountered my tribe at Oregon State University. I arrived there in the fall of 1971 to work as a post-doc in the ecosystem research program at the H. J. Andrews Experimental Forest. The Andrews is a beautiful forest ecosystem in the McKenzie River drainage where an NSF-funded Long-Term Ecological Research program had attracted a group of highly motivated, recently minted Ph.D.s. Our senior scientist leaders, including Jerry Franklin, were then in their thirties, full of energy, with ideas to share and an eagerness to contribute to research that would make the world a better place. The mix of disciplinary backgrounds was spectacular, from entomologists (affectionately known as "bug pickers") to fisheries biologists ("fish squeezers") to forest ecologists and geologists. Our rather scruffy crew of early-seventies longhairs was charged with the mundane task of collecting numbers on such things as nitrogen, carbon, water, and sediment. However, we quickly stumbled into unanticipated topics that turned out to be far more exciting and fruitful. For example, once we started to examine the role of dead wood in streams, we had to call on expertise from terrestrial and aquatic biology, forest and stream ecology, geomorphology, and other disciplines. Working at the interfaces of so many disciplines was challenging, exciting, and lots of fun. Our studies became some of the basic work in thinking about old-growth forests and how they function, but we didn't really set out to study old growth—we just followed our noses and made some interesting connections.

Engaging in storytelling at the Andrews Forest came naturally with this group. For me it was legitimized as a respectable way to do science when I read some of the eulogies and memorials to Robert MacArthur, an eminent ecologist who died in 1972. I was particularly taken by his attitude about publishing. In an article on MacArthur's work, Stephen Fretwell wrote, "In all research reporting, over-attention to detail can obscure the spirit of curiosity and wonder upon which good, basic research depends. MacArthur's work . . . makes inexcusable the report that is deadly dull, but otherwise correct. Better to spend (as MacArthur did) one's time and energy being interesting; if something has to be sacrificed, let it be exactness. Clearly, one can contribute as much with such an approach." I paraphrased this as a guiding mantra for scientific research: *What is the storyline?*

Communities of scientists sometimes coalesce into these intense group endeavors. I think of them as science "tribes," gatherings of motivated individuals sharing an excitement of discovery and a professional dedication to solid research heightened by a sense of shared purpose, rich camaraderie, and, I can only call it, *joie de vivre*. I don't choose the word tribe to imply exclusiveness, just that resonance and enthusiasm for learning about how the world works. The bonds of respect, friendship, and shared endeavor that are forged in such circumstances are among the greatest rewards of being a field scientist. For ecologists this tribalism is most strongly felt when focused on an interesting landscape.

So, at the Andrews Forest we got to do interesting work with interesting people in a beautiful place; and we learned a great deal about old-growth forests and streams. That work had substantial, mostly unanticipated impacts on science and forest management in subsequent decades. But, by the late 1970s the funding was tight and for personal and professional reasons I moved on to work in private forestry on an aquatic-ecology science team. The work was interesting, but the team was very small and we lacked a single, compelling landscape to rally around. I began to feel that I had lost my coordinates, and I missed that sense of working together to really understand how the system works.

Then the eruption of Mount St. Helens in 1980 brought the tribe together again. Shortly before the eruption I had joined the Pacific Northwest Research Station of the Forest Service and that organization helped champion and coordinate ecological studies at the volcano. Our "field pulses" at Mount St. Helens were incredibly exciting science "happenings" involving several hundred people from many agencies and universities. Despite the physical and mental exhaustion, science work at Mount St. Helens hardly seemed like work; it was too much fun and too charged with adrenalin. Flying in via helicopter to new places never before visited by humans offered us a deluge of intellectual challenges. We puzzled over peculiar new ecological and biogeochemical features, such as warm methane seeps far from the volcano, microbes living at the boiling temperature of water on the new volcanic dome, and the positive effects of erosion on vegetation establishment. Through frequent interactions with the media, we tried to convey to the public something of our excitement about these startling scientific discoveries. There seemed to be intense

worldwide interest in the conditions close to the volcano. Some
discoveries were rather worrisome, like finding the organisms
that cause Legionnaires disease flourishing in Spirit Lake, where
we sampled frequently. During this time, I experienced flu-like
symptoms similar to those of Legionnaires disease, but they could
have been just as easily due to the mental and physical fatigue of
those heady days of working at the volcano.

When I returned in the summer of 2005, twenty-five years after
the eruption, the land had been transformed again. The places
that had looked so raw in 1980 no longer looked that way to me.
The lakes had made remarkably rapid recovery in most respects,
especially in terms of water chemistry, which had returned to
pre-eruption conditions within a couple of years. Many streams
in the area of blast-toppled forest took on the character of pre-
eruption conditions within a decade or so. The forests, on the
other hand, are making a slow return in many areas where old-
growth forests once stood. But over all, what struck me most
forcefully in 2005 was the incredible exuberance of life.

The Mount St. Helens landscape of 2005 was still emotionally
charged for me, but in different ways. For more than a decade I'd
been working as a research administrator. I had not been doing
much actual science, and being out in the field again with some of
my old volcano friends and some remarkable writers who had a
knack for keen observation and clear expression, I felt once again
that sense of being part of a "tribe." It gave me the space to think
about what my whole Mount St. Helens experience had meant to
me, and where my life had gone since those earlier science-tribe
days.

By contrast, in my present position as a science administrator
of the Pacific Southwest Research Station, I oversee the work of
more than four hundred fifty people, but the relationships are
more structured and formal. Our efforts aren't focused deeply on
a specific locale, but are widely spread over California and across
the Pacific Islands. It is important work, I believe, but there is not
much sense of shared excitement, not much sense of tribe. The

job requires more restraint, more energy expended on finding a reasonable, balanced approach to how one says things, and less spontaneous reacting. Dealing with budgets and personnel issues, I find the enchantment missing, or at least very elusive. Sometimes I seem to be as isolated in my work as a lone conifer out on the Pumice Plain. In my career in science and in the Forest Service, I have wanted to make a difference, to have an impact that would last. The best way to do that, I've come to think, is to cultivate and support efforts to observe and interpret long-term ecological change using the tools of science, the arts, and whatever else can help. The resulting knowledge helps us live respectfully on the land and enjoy the pleasure of learning and sharing understanding. This means supporting places for long-term inquiry, places like the National Volcanic Monument and the Experimental Forests and Ranges. Anything we can do to bring together rich blends of people who are enchanted and curious about natural-world places and beings helps us to tell good stories about how the world works.

I want to help create a strong legacy of learning from the land, to foster places where others can experience that sense of shared learning, and together pass on the rich body of ecological knowledge we've accumulated. I want to help this knowledge find its way into management practices that are ever more respectful of the land. Going to the volcano with those writers and scientists and other volcano friends helped me reconnect with my own sense of purpose—to share the passion I feel for science, even for the *administration* of science! I thank Mount St. Helens for stepping into my life at key junctures to bring this purpose and passion into sharp focus.

Part IV

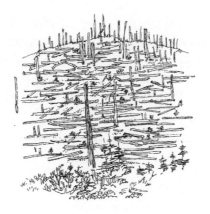

Two Stones

Scott Russell Sanders

A man turning sixty may lose perspective on time, seeing all
change as loss, counting his aches as if they were worry beads,
anticipating the chill wind of his last hour instead of breathing
in the present moment. And so, to regain his grip on time, to
console himself for loss, and to remind himself of the great story
in which he is taking part, he may consult with rocks. He is all
the more likely to do so if this man has been collecting pebbles
and cobbles and shards since he was a boy delving in the glacial
gravels of Ohio, and if, from his wide-ranging travels, he has
filled boxes and bowls on his writing desk with a menagerie of
stones.

In these days surrounding my sixtieth birthday, the two lumps
of rock I touch most frequently are both gritty and gray, and
each one fits comfortably in the palm of my hand. One of them
is over three hundred million years old; the other is less than half
my age. The older of the two is siltstone, plucked from a creek
bed near my home here in southern Indiana. It was laid down as
sediment in the shallow inland sea that flooded the central basin
of the North American plate for hundreds of millions of years.
Collisions between North America and other continental plates
have lifted up a series of mountain ranges where the Appalachians
now rise, each range in its youth towering as high as today's
Himalayas, and each one in turn eroding away under the friction
of ice and rain and wind. Some 320 million years ago, fragments
from one of those earlier mountain ranges tumbled down rivers
until the bits were ground finer than sand, and the slurry of grit
was flushed into the inland sea, where it settled to the bottom,
mixed with the fallen husks of marine creatures, and eventually
hardened into the scaly siltstone I hold in my hand.

The fossilized shapes in my stone are mostly crinoids, animals long abundant and now long extinct, with a slender stem and a flower-like mouth, more reminiscent of lilies than of their true relatives, the sea urchins and starfish. The stem was a column made up of flat, round segments, each with a hole in the center, like a washer. In crinoid fossils, these segments often appear singly, sometimes in short stacks, rarely as intact bodies, yet each of these fragments once formed part of a whole creature, every cell attuned to every other cell, as fully alive in its moment as I am in mine. Even though my sample of siltstone is young compared to the age of Earth, and even younger compared to the universe, measured on a human scale it is incomprehensibly old. To curl my fingers around a third of a billion years is comforting, for it reminds me that everything flows, mountains as well as rivers, entire species flourishing and perishing, the hardest rock yielding as surely as a man's bones.

☾ ☾ ☾

The younger of the two stones I handle most often these days is rough, angular, and surprisingly light, as filled with holes as a sponge. When rubbed, it gives off the faint smell of wood ash. It's a glassy mineral called pumice, which volcanoes have been making since Earth was new. This particular piece was formed just over twenty-five years ago, on May 18, 1980, when Mount St. Helens erupted.

I collected my chunk of pumice this past summer from the shore of Ghost Lake, which is ten or eleven miles northeast of Mount St. Helens, on the edge of the devastated area known as the blast zone. Some twenty of us were camping for a few days on a ridge overlooking the crater, mostly writers, photographers, and scientists who hoped to gain from this ravaged and recovering landscape, and from one another, insights into the ways of healing. We had been drawn together by our curiosity about the volcano and also, I came to realize, by a shared grief over the damage humans are inflicting on the planet, on other species, and

on our own kind. We all knew that the burning of oil and other
fossil fuels was destabilizing Earth's climate, even as our nation
waged war in the Middle East to assure the continued flow of
oil; we knew that the industrial economy was stripping topsoil
from the Midwest, emptying aquifers under the Great Plains,
felling rainforests in Alaska and Brazil, drilling in the Arctic
Refuge, poisoning the Gulf of Mexico, and emptying the seas
of fish, while pundits and merchants kept urging us to consume
ever more. We ached not only from these large losses but also
from the wrecking of our home places, the neighborhoods and
watersheds we loved.

It was a relief to visit the slopes of Mount St. Helens, where
humans bore no responsibility for the wreckage. We spent our
first day together learning from scientists who had studied the
landscape since the eruption about how life has returned with
surprising swiftness to the lakes, the shattered forests, and even
the desolate plain of pumice below the crater's lip. A quarter
century after the eruption, you can still walk among the silvery
trunks of downed or standing dead trees, mile after mile of
them, yet these carcasses have become hosts for new life, from
beetles to woodpeckers. The lakes and rivers have regained their
full complement of organisms. The violet blossoms of lupine,
red bristles of Indian paintbrush, pink spikes of fireweed, and
white buttons of pearly everlasting glimmer from the ashy soil.
Everywhere the saplings of noble fir, silver fir, Douglas fir, and
alder have begun to rise. Over the next century or so, if the
mountain remains quiet, the trees will return. For the present,
however, there is a greater diversity of life in this mosaic of
habitats than there was in the old-growth forest that preceded
the eruption.

This hopeful history kept our grief at bay until the second
evening, when we sat around the campfire trading memories and
songs. As the light faded, a trio of nighthawks cruised above
us, calling and feeding, and Mount St. Helens turned rosy with
alpenglow. Every little while, steam rose from the fumarole, so

obviously like puffs of breath that nobody bothered to make the comparison. It was easy to understand why tribes that had lived near the volcano for generations called it Loowit, meaning Fire Mountain or Smoking Mountain, and why they told stories about the Cascade peaks now and again quarreling with one another, shaking the ground, hurling rocks and trees. The Earth felt so alive in this place, we could forget for a while the devastation of other places.

Then someone told a story about the cutting of a grove of trees where he had sought refuge as a boy, another told about the young people of her tribe losing touch with their ancestral ways, a third told about an oil spill, and a fourth person, trying to speak, began to sob, a sound that seemed to well up from our common reservoir of sorrow.

Sparks rose from the fire, drawing my gaze upward into the black sky. I blinked and blinked, but it was a long while before I could make out the stars.

& & &

The next morning, several of us walked to Ghost Lake through a labyrinth of blown down and standing dead trees. These enormous, whitened hulks were mostly Douglas fir that had flourished here for five hundred years, since the last time the volcano had scourged this area. We paused along the path to nibble huckleberries and praise the fireweed. Our arrival at the edge of the lake alarmed a spotted sandpiper whose chicks were feeding in the shallows. The mother bird circled above us, crying, until we drew back from the shore, and then she swooped down, gathered her chicks, and led them to safety in a thicket of willows. A song sparrow perched atop a cattail whistling notes I knew from my Indiana backyard. The spires of a young forest, as dense as fur, thrust up among dead trees on the surrounding slopes. In the daylight, loss no longer seemed to be the last word.

As we turned away from Ghost Lake, I stopped at the base of an eroding bank to examine a heap of talus, mostly bits of pumice no larger than a child's marbles. My eye snagged on a bigger piece that was riddled with holes, the imprints of hot gases from the 1980 eruption. Only when I picked up the stone and held it close did I see that the pores on top, where sunshine and rain could reach them, were filled with moss. The vibrant green tufts seemed to flicker up like tiny flames from the sterile rock.

One isn't supposed to remove anything from the Volcanic National Monument, but I persuaded myself that this lump of pumice, no larger than a hen's egg, could serve the cause of conservation by helping me tell the story of nature's recuperative power. So I put the stone in my pocket and carried it home.

          ⅊ ⅊ ⅊

Over the following months, I used my two stones to illustrate talks I gave around the country. The 320 million-year-old chunk of siltstone, a compound of mountain dust and seawater, served as a reminder of Earth's great age and relentless flow and perennial vigor. Portions of our own DNA, I pointed out, could be traced back to the crinoids whose lithe bodies, broken into fragments, were packed together in this fossil as richly as raisins and dates in a fruitcake. The siltstone also helped me speak about my home on the planet, this Indiana hill country sculpted by water from ancient seafloor, the lowlands lush with horsetail and sycamore and fern, the uplands shaded by maples, hickories, beeches, and oaks, and lit up by wildflowers.

Using my pumice as a prop, I told audiences what I had learned from observing the dance of desolation and renewal on the flanks of Mount St. Helens. The swift recovery of this devastated landscape showed just how resilient nature is—how inventive, persistent, and sly. It showed that the Earth, like our own flesh, is capable of mending itself. This wasn't to suggest that we should remain passive in the face of injuries, especially those that we ourselves had caused—climate disruption, habitat destruction, extinction of species, poisoning of air and water and soil—but rather that in seeking to slow down, eventually halt, and partially undo this damage, we could draw on the healing power of nature.

In telling about my discovery of moss flickering up like green flames from holes in the pumice, I recalled the wonder expressed by William Blake in response to life's miraculous energy:

> Tyger! Tyger! burning bright
> In the forests of the night,
> What immortal hand or eye
> Could frame thy fearful symmetry?
> In what distant deeps or skies
> Burnt the fire of thine eyes?

I recalled Aldo Leopold's account of how he joined in the shooting of a mother wolf, and then underwent a profound change of heart as he watched "a fierce green fire dying in her eyes." "I realized then," Leopold wrote, "and have known ever since, that there was something new to me in those eyes—something known only to her and to the mountain. I was young then, and full of trigger-itch; I thought that because fewer wolves meant more deer, that no wolves would mean hunters' paradise. But after seeing the green fire die, I sensed that neither the wolf nor the mountain agreed with such a view." I wanted my listeners not just to know but to *feel* that the green fire burning in wolf or tiger or moss burns in each of us, animates and shapes us, links us in kinship to all living things. I wanted others to undergo the change described by Leopold, a conversion from thoughtless exploiter to devoted caretaker of Earth's bounty.

&ear; &ear; &ear;

In between trips, I returned the siltstone to my writing desk, but I set the pumice among other mossy rocks in a damp and shady spot behind our house. If the local moss was happy there, I figured, the moss from the skirts of Loowit ought to thrive as well. With each trip, however, the green sparks in the pores of the rock grew dimmer, becoming harder and harder to see even with a magnifying glass, and eventually they guttered out. No combination of moisture and sunlight would revive them. And so my symbol of life's resilience became a symbol of life's fragility, or perhaps of its elegant adaptation to the conditions of a particular place. My stone was out of place; it belonged back on the talus pile next to Ghost Lake, downwind from the volcano.

For now I keep the chunk of pumice on my writing desk, occasionally picking it up, running my fingers over the rough surface, gazing into the holes that seem as lifeless as craters on the moon. If my travels should carry me back to Mount St. Helens, I will take the stone with me and replace it. I will hang onto the siltstone, for it belongs here, on this old patch of seabed we call Indiana. Between them, the two stones, young and old, remind me that Earth is restless, powerful, forever casting up new materials and forms. A sixty-year-old man is merely one of those ephemeral shapes, his passage all the more precious to him for being so brief. I feel a reverence for this wild, creative, mysterious flow of things. Our lives, our civilization, everything we can touch or imagine is part of that flow, a wave lifted for a moment above the current, and then drawn back to the source.

Regardless of what we do, Earth will go on about its business, as demonstrated by the ancient history of rising and disintegrating mountains and the recent history of the land surrounding Mount St. Helens. We cannot save the world, for it is not ours to save; the best we can do is to honor its magnificent energy. If we value the living abundance that we all inherited at our birth, then we should do everything we can to preserve it. In this work of preservation and healing we are allied with nature itself, which holds no grudges, never becomes discouraged, and never grows old. Amid so many wounds, this knowledge keeps me humble, keeps me playful and hopeful, keeps me sane.

Nature's Shaking Keeps Me Steady

Susan Zwinger and Ann Zwinger

My mother, Ann Zwinger, has always been the consummate desert and river rat. Yet she was excited to join a distinguished group of scientists, writers, and philosophers to examine Mount St. Helens, Washington's most active volcano, in the summer of 2005. As she packed her gear for the trip, she wrote:

> *I often find that new ways of looking at the world are engendered by new places, as if the old underpinnings are not there as crutches, and that's how I feel about going to Mount St. Helens. There are things roiling around in my mind that have become more bothersome in the last year and perhaps … a strange place with strange winds and sounds and feel will help me get them straight.*

On the first evening of that adventure, she sat on a ridge just a few miles from the crater and wrote:

> *Jerry Franklin's insistence that Mount St. Helens' eruption was not a catastrophe but "nature as usual" so appeals to me, because that's the natural world I know. But it isn't what most people I talk to know—it was a catastrophe. When are we going to stretch our minds beyond our meager lifetimes and see the warming and cooling of a planet in transition happened many times, and many volcanoes belched fire and coated the walls of the Grand Canyon with extravagant columns of basalt. I still come across people who believe spiders are insects. Who don't know the parts of a flower. Who are simply ignorant about the natural world and worse, not interested …*

When I wrote Beyond the Aspen Grove *thirty-five
years ago, I was warmed and astonished by the number of
letters that told of how the writer enjoyed nature because
they had been introduced to that world by their parents,
something that had never occurred to me because it had
been a small part and accepted part of my growing up,
and learning about our forty acres in the mountains was
simply an extension without the mosquitoes and heat and
humidity of an Indiana summer. ...*

*I sensed a lack of connection with the natural world I'd
not seen before. One student wrote about sleeping out for
the first time in her life, a good essay but not particularly
natural history ~ she was focusing inward rather than
outward. Then this spring Richard Louv's* Last Child in
the Woods *came out and pieces started to fall together.
The generation of parents who now have children in
college has been one in which there has been perhaps more
emphasis on getting and spending, late and soon, managed
childhood, all the pop words we're hearing about us.
My epiphany came when I realized that the students I'm
teaching now are different and the difference is that there
weren't as many parents to put a small hand in theirs and
watch a dragonfly emerge, giggle at water striders, talk
about beavers building their dam across the pond, answer
"What is this?" and the endless "Why?"*

On November 9, 2005, three months after she camped on
Mount St. Helens, Ann Zwinger suffered a serious stroke. Her
mind, like volcanic lava, is still there, but churning underground.
Now I have come to the mountain to try to understand this
catastrophe. Last night, I slept in a clear-cut high on a hill close to
the Monument boundary. It was very cold all night, with blurry,
quivering light strips across a clear sky full of stars. In the darkest
of times, my eye began to see strange things—bright ribbons
glowing eerily from a nearby slash pile. When I arose in the

predawn freeze to examine these strips of wood, I remembered how strands of *Armellaria mellea* glowed in the dark, so brightly that lumberyards in England covered their woodpiles during World War II for fear that the fungi's light would attract bombing raids. Soldiers stuck fragments of wood with glowing mycelia on their helmets so that they would not run into each other in the trenches.

This morning, I sit here with three feet of Kalama ash under me, thinking not of pyroclastics, but of water—water's great force in sculpting and resculpting the land. I am here above four thousand feet on Windy Ridge at Ryan Lake, only fifteen miles from the Mount St. Helens crater. Just twenty-five years ago, a blast of 572-degree ash traveling three hundred miles per hour flattened all the trees on hills facing the crater and charred three campers sleeping here. Now ducks and shorebirds gurgle; passerines twitter. How quickly life comes back in water. Past violence breeds beauty. Immanuel Kant spoke of beauty and terror, of horrendous power and multiplicity creating awe. This fall morning, the reflections of young trees—brilliant greens of alder, golds of willows, red-orange of vine maples—are beautifully distorted in Ryan Lake, recasting past violence into Impressionist painting. Beyond the lake, against the somber background of gray ash quilted by a black linearity of tree trunks, shafts of sun penetrate the clouds and run like spotlights across the vibrant fall ridge.

I am focused on water, not on pyroclastics, because water is my mother's great love: fresh water, the rivers and the lakes. Squatting here on the northwest shoulder of an active, steaming volcano this morning, I feel firsthand how much volcanic activity has shaped our landscapes and our very existence on earth. Some scientists believe that life may have begun in a volcanic setting, that the heat and chemistry set off chain reactions that turned methane, ammonia, and hydrogen into amino acids, into proteins, into complex polymers—which then organized themselves into structures capable of metabolism. Reproducing beings! I have no trouble believing this on Ryan Lake.

On this glorious fall morning, as brilliant colors lash the ash-dark background, I believe in life's resilience. I breathe deeply, imagining the dynasty of anaerobic microbes, which ate the oxygen and created stinking lake soups. This morning I believe in the refreshing rains, snows, groundwater, and tricklets falling into these lakes to dilute the organics, restoring them to normal oxygen levels. Ryan Lake is now teeming with life: salamanders, fish, insects, and frogs. A red salamander on a gray log, reeds and rushes hiding duck nests along the margins. I believe in the simple power of streams, which cut down through nine feet of ash to the organic soil, bringing up buried seeds still viable years later.

Down the mountain, vestiges of waterfalls, roaring mudflows, ice fragments blown from the high glaciers have left a rippled and pitted land, as strange as the moon, as familiar as a freshly tilled garden.

Water in a volcano is like no water we know from our taps. The power of water buried in the subduction zone is highly compacted, laced with heavy metals, and gassed with hydrogen sulfide. The atomic weight of heavy water from vents and volcanoes is a sneak peak into our mysterious mantle. What goes on in Earth's mind and how? We in the land of Mount St. Helens are constantly aware of subterranean mysteries. The children of Cowlitz County will never be oblivious to nature. Cowlitz citizens have learned to read the steam rising from the mountain as an indicator of the volcano's mood. The more sulfuric belches, the more trouble we can expect. How my mother would enjoy this display of scientific savvy from the tire repairman, who asked me, does this steam come from a rising fist of molten lava and melted ocean crust explosive as hydrogen bombs, or has it trickled down from rain and melting glaciers?

Last fall I climbed the north flank of Mount Baker, another active volcano, against a deep blue, clear sky. I was shocked to see thick cumulus rising up from the southwest fumarole with not a cloud in the sky. If Mount Baker blows, my home on a nearby island could be buried by lahars.

Down the tiny logging road from Windy Ridge I pause at vertical layers of colorful ash: black to red to gray in patchworks. Giant tree molds fallen and flamed out in the lava have left long tube hollows, which now harbor moisture and a miniature world of plants. Northern gophers dig down, pop up to eat grass seeds, stitching together surface and earth. As Ann Zwinger would do, I turn from the macrocosm to the exquisite microcosm. How carefully she taught me to search out the wonders in the land. An orange lichen uses the nitrogen from urine: *Xanthoria elegans*. *Tubifera ferruginosa* embedded with the red lipsticks—fruiting bodies—delights me. Mount St Helens' microcosm creates the fractals on which the macrocosm expands.

John Muir wrote that the water ouzel is completely part of the streams he inhabits. A mother who lives so thoroughly on rivers is shaped by the places she has rowed, paddled, and ridden. Ann Zwinger is like the creatures that live in the fastest of currents, who have evolved a resplendent array of claws, grapples, hooks, and toes to cling to the rocks. She will cling to life. And not just this: she will recover. Her recovery will parallel the biological force, which is so rapidly returning Mount St. Helens to her green self on top of the thick ash and ravaged river drainages. Such metaphors do not lessen our loss, but Nature's shaking keeps me steady.

What if I Chose?

Kim Stafford

What if I chose, said alder, to only do what only I can do?
What if I chose, said penstemon, to only do what gives me joy?
What if I chose, said coyote, to take in one quick bite
      what gives me joy, and what only I can do:
      a song that raises thunder in the human heart?

What if I chose, said silver fir, to only fall as seed
      where the wind wills?
What if I chose, said fireweed, to follow through
      disturbance into Eden?
What if I chose, said someone small, to hide my cache
      of seed on the pumice plain?

What if I chose—by seeing and receiving, by singing
      and believing—to be a human being?

What if I chose, said the western toad, to come down
      over snow at night to find my native pool?
What if I chose, said the dormant bud beneath the bark,
      to unfurl my little flag?

What if—so schooled by water, stone, flower, and tree—
      I chose to be a human being?
Then I would be chosen to do what only I can do.
I would be chosen to only do what gives me joy.
Friends, you may glimpse me now and then.

Languages of Volcanic Landscapes

Frederick J. Swanson

As a young geologist in 1980, I felt a powerful attraction to volcanoes, and I thought I knew volcanoes rather well. I had studied volcanology. I had climbed volcanic peaks in the Cascades. And I had tried to be an attentive citizen of my volcanic region, the Pacific Northwest. But when I had a chance to go with other scientists to Mount St. Helens within days of its May 18th, 1980, eruption, that all changed. I stepped out of a helicopter into the dust and mist of the blasted landscape, and I could barely comprehend where I was. Everything was gray in the normally green Pacific Northwest landscape. Muddy geysers erupted on the newly formed Pumice Plain below, and the volcano responsible for this chaos was hidden in clouds. The helicopter radio passed on messages of continuing harmonic tremor, signaling possible further eruptive activity. My preconceptions of how volcanic landscapes behave in the aftermath of an eruption were blown away like the top of St. Helens, and I've been reconstructing my understanding ever since.

From that day forward my engagement with volcanoes has only intensified. I eagerly follow the latest developments in geology and ecology, but I've also become interested in cultural responses to eruptive landscapes, to the ways in which societies and their languages adapt to living with volcanoes. It has been fascinating to think about the many ways we speak about volcanoes: we use the scientific language of volcanology, of course, but also a language of ecological responses to volcanism, and a language of human engagement with volcanic landscapes. Culture permeates each of these languages.

Cataclysmic volcanic events profoundly change cultures and ecosystems, testing our emotional reactions and our language.

Where volcanic events have become familiar, they have spawned technical terms of cultural origin. This geological language of volcanoes has become part of our general vocabulary, and finds a place in the language of poets as well as scientists. The language of human and ecological responses to change commonly carries a sense of personal, corporate, and public values—intended or unintended. Mount St. Helens is a great place to reflect on these intersections of volcanoes, culture, and language.

Some Volcano Vocabulary

Volcanoes ring the globe and erupt in many ways and in many cultures. This cosmopolitan setting of volcanism produces a global etymology for the vocabulary of volcanic landforms, materials, and processes. Much of the technical language of volcanology was born in culture, not science. Some terms are obscure and opaque; others evocative. A few examples reveal the richness of this language and its cultural roots.

"Mudflow" is a common descriptive term for the rapidly moving slurries of water, sediment, boulders, and trees that flow from the flanks of volcanoes and down river channels. But volcanologists are more likely to use the Indonesian (Javanese) term "lahar" for volcanic mudflows. A colloquial Chinese term for mudflow translates as "sludge dragon"—a roiling, coiling, and dangerous beast, an appropriate image, since lahars kill more people than other volcanic processes.

A "pyroclastic flow" is a rapid, turbulent flow of exceedingly hot gasses, ash, and rock fragments. The French, who have studied such processes at volcanoes in French colonies, such as Soufriere Hills on Montserrat, call them "nuée ardentes" or "glowing avalanches." Pyroclastic flows occurred repeatedly at Mount St. Helens in 1980, and piled up at the foot of the north flank, forming the Pumice Plain. Like lahars, pyroclastic flows are fast and very dangerous volcanic processes.

Any fine-grained volcanic material that falls from the sky is commonly and casually called "ash," but to a volcanologist this term is restricted to particles less than 0.08 inches (2 mm) in diameter. The Greek word "tephra" is the more general term for any volcanic debris—particles big or small—fallen from the sky. A common style of eruption producing tephra of widely ranging particle size is the violent "Plinian" type, named for the Roman Pliny the Younger on the basis of his deliberate description of the explosive eruption of Mt. Vesuvius that inundated Pompeii in AD 79. The Italian term "lapilli" refers to tephra ranging in diameter from 0.04 to 2.52 inches. My favorite tephra term is "accretionary lapilli," which are little spheres of very fine ash stuck to water droplets, forming mudballs of the lapilli size class. Accretionary lapilli formed in the climactic Mount St. Helens eruption when the finest ash in the dust cloud produced by the blast collected on water droplets condensed from the steam that drove the blast. I got an up-close and a bit too personal view of these mudballs as they splattered on the windscreen of our helicopter during that May 28, 1980, foray to Mount St. Helens. As the ash drifted northeastward with the wind, accretionary lapilli formed and fell to the earth, blanketing the landscape with a layer up to nearly an inch thick. This distinctive deposit impeded the flow of water into the soil and the exchange of gases between soil and atmosphere, contributing to the death of many old-growth fir trees in areas northeast of the volcano.

Lava flows are perhaps the most common image of a volcanic process, but none occurred in the 1980 eruption of Mount St. Helens. The black, fluid lava of Hawaiian volcanoes sculpts fascinating forms in rock and glass. The sharp, clinkery rubble surface of an "a'a" lava flow or the smooth, ropy-textured surface of a "pahoehoe" flow invoke a sense of the exclamations barefoot Hawaiians might have uttered walking across them, perhaps giving the different surfaces their names. One is treacherous, the other provides easy traveling.

Hawaii is also the source of the term "Pele's hair," the fine, golden glass threads of cooled lava spun from blobs of lava thrown into the air during a fountaining eruption of very fluid, incandescent magma. The small blobs themselves may take the form of teardrops termed "Pele's tears." Pele is the Hawaiian goddess of fire, lightning, and volcanoes.

The language born in these various cultures is widely used because mudflows, eruptions of tephra, and lava flows are common globally where volcanic events occur. Our language for very infrequent volcanic events is more clinical, less settled, and perhaps less interesting. Giant landslides occur in the lifetime of many high, steep-sided stratovolcanoes characteristic of some volcanic chains such as the Cascade Range, but are rare in recorded history. Massive volcanic landslides take on many names, such as "debris avalanche," "rock avalanche," and "sector collapse," indicating that a major chunk of a volcano, including the summit, breaks loose and flows out onto the surrounding terrain. The landslide instrumental in triggering the 1980 eruption of Mount St. Helens—two-thirds of a cubic mile of mountain top—was the largest landslide ever observed on earth. But it was only a tenth the size of one that eviscerated Mount Shasta three hundred thousand years ago.

Huge volcanic blasts, such as the one heralding the eruption of Mount St. Helens, are also rare in human history and probably in geological history as well. Consequently, the terminology is unsettled, even disputed, among specialists who each have their own ways of interpreting the process and, hence, the appropriate, literal terminology. Even within a single geological report documenting the 1980 activity of Mount St. Helens, this single event was referred to as the "directed blast," "pyroclastic density flow," "pyroclastic surge," and simply "blast."

These examples suggest that the language for volcanoes and their self-constructive and self-destructive processes may have strongest cultural undertones where a culture has experienced numerous volcanic events or where chronicles of volcanic eruptions have had lasting impact. The language for volcanic processes that are rare, especially in parts of the globe without deep written histories, may be sparse. For these, it may fall to the science community to settle on a vocabulary, and the wrangling over terminology may go on for decades.

Language of Ecological Responses to Eruptions

How do we react to, think about, and discuss a landscape transformed by violent volcanic eruption? The scientific language of volcanology attempts to be descriptive, avoiding, as much as possible, references to human values, and in this it has some parallels with language used to describe ecological responses to big disturbances, such as volcanic eruptions; but there are also some important differences between geological and ecological vocabularies. Our language for processes of ecological change, employing terms such as *succession, immigration, survival,* and *competitive interactions,* is intended to be descriptive, though we can sense strong anthropomorphic hints in these terms. Human values appear clearly in descriptions of initial effects of the disturbances and prescriptions for management of ecological change thereafter.

Right after the 1980 eruption of Mount St. Helens ecologists and the news media spoke of "the devastated area," "the zone of devastation," "a moonscape." But, soon, surviving organisms and surprising pioneers appeared. It became clear that there were both winners and losers, ecologically speaking—some species had their numbers eliminated or greatly reduced while others found new opportunities to flourish. Ecologists developed a more nuanced understanding of the volcanic impacts, and their language followed. The single devastation zone came to be seen as separate disturbance zones with distinctive properties—the down-tree part of the blast zone, the standing-dead or scorch zone, and the pumice plain of pyroclastic flow deposits where ecological development had to begin essentially from scratch. Ecologists began to avoid the hot language of "devastation" for the greening landscape, and to focus more on the nuanced "responses" of ecosystems to the disturbance.

More *pre*scriptive terms concern notions of where ecosystems had been in the past and where they may be headed. What are the relevance and meanings of the terms "recovery," "reestablishment," and "restoration" in a place of such profound change? What can we hope to restore, what should we not, what can we not? Responses to these questions depend on our attitudes about nature and our place in the world. Initial expectations that we would observe ecological "recovery" and could direct "restoration" to pre-disturbance conditions gave way to the realization that the path of ecological change in natural systems was quite different from human efforts to restore forests, lakes, and streams. For systems permitted to develop without human intervention, each spot on the landscape was on its own path, and pre-1980 conditions were probably not their destination. The notion of "recovery" may be relevant to specific components of an ecosystem in specific parts of the Mount St. Helens landscape, such as certain fish species in lakes where both the lake and the fish existed before the 1980 eruption. But some parts of the landscape are new places on the face of the Earth—the crater, new lakes, and the debris avalanche deposit, which raised the land surface up to six hundred feet in places. "Restoration" and "recovery" are not taking place there—these are wholly new ecological systems.

Concepts of recovery and restoration in greatly altered landscapes raise very challenging questions. Where should we plant trees, put fish in lakes, or alter stream channels in the name of ecological recovery, commodity production, or our perception of doing good deeds? This comes down to a matter of personal values, which may be expressed through corporate and government actions. In the blast zone of Mount St. Helens the timber industry quickly "salvaged" dead trees and planted a new forest, and the U.S. Forest Service did likewise on some federal lands. But Congress established the first-ever National Volcanic Monument, directing that natural processes should "proceed substantially unimpeded." So now vigorous, young tree plantations grow on one side of the boundary of the Monument, and on the other side stands a complex ecosystem with shrubs, herbs, scattered trees, and diverse assemblages of animals. Which is right, which is wrong? Which good, which bad? In America we possess a wealth of space, so we can often have it both ways and learn from the differences.

Personal Language of Volcanic Landscapes

Thus, we reside in several layers of volcanic culture—the global scientific knowledge and language of volcanoes, the experience of the 1980 eruption of Mount St. Helens shared across today's cultures, and the cultural conflicts over responses to eruptions. In the Mount St. Helens volcanic landscape we can sense the presence of volcanoes in broad cultural terms, and also in strictly personal terms. We have engagements of fear, curiosity, neighborliness, respect, awe. In the myths of Native people of this region, whose cultures have resided here for millennia—long enough to experience many eruptions—volcanoes are battling gods, or wooing lovers. In contemporary society, as Ursula LeGuin has observed, Portlanders ask, "Is the volcano out today?" in reference to viewing our neighbors Mount St. Helens and Mount Hood.

My strongest feelings for volcanoes have no vocabulary. Whether I'm teetering at the lip of a crater rim, so wild and unstable no person should be there, or standing on a huge boulder facing directly up into the crater, or caught up in a moment of silence viewing the snow peak from my home sixty miles away, I come to the edge of language. I look to see what the volcano has to say today—cloud cap or wisp of steam from the dome or trail of dust from rockfall on the crater wall, or silence. The power and the presence are beyond words.

Part V

Pearly Everlasting

Gary Snyder

Walk a trail down to the lake
mountain ash and elderberries red
old-growth log bodies blown about,
whacked down, tumbled in the new ash *wadis.*
Root-mats tipped up, veiled in tall straight fireweed,
fields of prone logs laid by blast
in-line north-south down and silvery
limbless barkless poles—
clear to the alpine ridgetop all you see
is toothpicks of dead trees
thousands of summers
at detritus-cycle rest
—hard and dry in the sun—the long life of the down tree yet to go
bedded in bushes of pearly everlasting
dense white flowers
saplings of bushy vibrant silver fir
the creek here once was "Harmony Falls"
The pristine mountain
just a little battered now
the smooth dome gone
ragged crown

the lake was shady *yin*—
now blinding water mirror of the sky
remembering days of fir and hemlock—
no blame to magma or the mountain
& sit on a clean down log at the lake's edge,
the water dark as tea.

I had asked Mt. St. Helens for help
the day I climbed it,   so seems she did
The trees all lying flat like,   after that big party
Siddhartha went to on the night he left the house for good,
crowd of young friends whipped from sexy dancing
dozens crashed out on the floor

angelic boys and girls, sleeping it off.
A palace orgy of the gods but what
"we" see is "Blast Zone" sprinkled with
clustered white flowers

"Do not be tricked by human-centered views," says Dogen,
And Siddhartha looks it over, slips away—for another forest—
—to really get right down on life and death.

If you ask for help it comes.
But not in any way you'd ever know
—thank you Loowit, lawilayt-lá, *Smoky Mâ*
              gracias   xiexie   grace

For Further Reading

Bishop, Ellen Morris, *In Search of Ancient Oregon: A Geological and Natural History* (**Timber Press, 2004**). Bishop is a top-notch writer, photographer, and interpreter of geology. The geologic history of this slice of the planet is simply astonishing.

Calderazzo, John, *Rising Fire: Volcanoes and Our Inner Lives* (**Lyons, 2004**). How do different cultures respond to the volcanoes in their midst? Calderazzo traveled around the world to explore volcanoes on the land and in the mind.

Dale, Virginia, Frederick J. Swanson, Charlie Crisafulli, eds., *Ecological Responses to the 1980 Eruption of Mount St. Helens* (**Springer, 2005**). Fifty scientists, 25 years of ecological studies on the mountain: geology and ecology; forests, lakes, and streams; amphibians, small mammals, and lupines; even rotting rodents.

Eiseley, Loren, *The Immense Journey* (**Random House, 1957**). Eiseley was one of those rare people who see evolution happening all around them. A masterful writer, his gift is to show us how to imagine and to think materially about vast reaches of time.

Lopez, Barry, and Debra Gwartney, eds., *Home Ground: Language for an American Landscape* (**Trinity University Press, 2006**). Where language meets landscape, the editors invited forty-five of the country's most land-savvy writers to create what one reviewer calls, "etymological landforms," sometimes lyrical, always insightful evocations of place. Original and timely.

McPhee, John, *Annals of the Former World* (**Farrar Straus Giroux, 1998**). McPhee found a number of contemporary geologists who were also great storytellers, and he listened to them with wonder, curiosity, and keen intelligence. His Pulitzer-prize-winning collection brought geology into our living rooms.

Savoy, Lauret E., Eldridge M. Moores, and Judith E. Moores, eds., *Bedrock: Writers on the Wonders of Geology* (**Trinity University Press, 2006**). Deep time; earthquakes and faults; volcanoes and eruptions; mountains and deserts; the flow of ice—*Bedrock* gathers fiction, poetry, and nonfiction writings that scan the geological horizons of Earth.

Snyder, Gary, *Danger on Peaks* (**Shoemaker & Hoard, 2004**). Snyder's supple poems pay tribute to Mount St. Helens, from his first sight of Spirit Lake at age thirteen and first ascent at fifteen to post-eruption visits. A compelling, insightful work.

Winchester, Simon, *Krakatoa: The Day the Earth Exploded – Aug. 27, 1883* (**Harper Collins, 2003**). Winchester's account of the cataclysmic eruption of Krakatoa blends science and adventure to portray both the physical events—explosive eruptions, tsunamis, dust circling the hemisphere—and their effects on the people and arts of Java.

Contributors

Gary Braasch has been taking of photographs of Mount St. Helens' landscapes for more than three decades. He is an Ansel Adams Award-winning photojournalist, and the author of *Photographing the Patterns of Nature* and coauthor of *Secrets of the Old-Growth Forest*, and *Entering the Grove*. He is a frequent contributor to magazines including *Time, US News and World Report, Smithsonian, Natural History,* and many others. His latest book is *Earth Under Fire: How Global Warming Is Changing the World.*

John Calderazzo is the author of *Rising Fire: Volcanoes and Our Inner Lives*, a multi-disciplinary look at the many ways in which volcanoes around the world have affected human culture. An English professor who has taught creative nonfiction writing at Colorado State University since 1986, Calderazzo has received a Colorado Council on the Arts Creative Nonfiction Fellowship and has been nominated for the Pushcart Prize. His other books include *Writing from Scratch: Freelancing*, and a children's science book, *101 Questions About Volcanoes*. John was voted a "Best CSU Teacher" in 1998.

Writer and calligrapher **Christine Colasurdo** is the author of *Return to Spirit Lake: Journey through a Lost Landscape,* a "Washington Reads" recommended book. She has given talks in California, Oregon, and Washington and has created three exhibits about the volcano: "Spirit Lake Remembered," "Hiking the Harmony Trail," and "In the Land of Loowit." Colasurdo has led tours to the volcano and has been a guest twice on National Public Radio's "Science Friday." Her work has appeared in *Sierra, Audubon,* and *Orion Magazine*, and she is the author of *Golden Gate National Parks*. She is also a tireless volunteer working to protect Mount St. Helens from mining, logging, and road-building.

Charlie Crisafulli, research ecologist with the USDA Forest Service, has been conducting ecological studies around Mount St. Helens for twenty-seven years, and plans to continue for years to come. He has spent over fifteen hundred days and nights on the land investigating the ecological responses of small mammals, birds, amphibians, arthropods, plants, and fungi to the 1980 eruption, and has published numerous articles and book chapters on these topics. In his free time, he regularly visits the mountain with his family and friends to ski, snowshoe, fish, hike, photograph, harvest mushrooms and huckleberries, and watch wildlife.

John Daniel set chokers for the Weyerhaeuser Timber Company off Spirit Lake Highway, within sight of Mount St. Helens, in the spring of 1969. He climbed the mountain once before it blew, and learned of its eruption when a pickup-load of ash arrived at a gas station across the street from his residence in La Grande, Oregon, where he then urged schoolchildren to write volcano poems. *Rogue River Journal*, winner of a 2006 Pacific Northwest Booksellers Award, is his most recent book. He lives in the non-volcanic Coast Range north of Noti, Oregon.

Growing up in Camas, Washington, **Jerry Franklin** could see Mount St. Helens from his home. He began conducting research at Mount St. Helens as a scientist for the USDA Forest Service, Pacific Northwest Research Station, in 1959, and facilitated terrestrial research projects following the 1980 eruption. He continues to study and write about ecosystem development in the post-eruption landscape. Professor of Ecosystem Analysis at the College of Forest Resources, University of Washington, Franklin has been recognized for his contributions to science and conservation by The Wilderness Society, American Forests, and the Society for Conservation Biology, among many others, and has received a Heinz Foundation Award for his work on old-growth forests.

Charles Goodrich was backpacking twelve miles southeast of Mount St. Helens when it erupted on May 18, 1980. Six years later, he climbed by full moonlight to the lip of the steaming crater with his soon-to-be wife, arriving just at sunrise. Goodrich is the author of a volume of poems, *Insects of South Corvallis*, and a collection of essays about nature, parenting, and building his own house, *The Practice of Home*. Having worked for twenty-five years as a professional gardener, he now serves as the Program Director for the Spring Creek Project for Ideas, Nature, and the Written Word at Oregon State University.

Robin Wall Kimmerer, an enrolled member of the Citizen Band Potawatomi, is the author of *Gathering Moss: A Natural and Cultural History* (John Burroughs Medal winner). A professor of plant ecology whose research includes the ecology of mosses and the role of traditional ecological knowledge in ecological restoration, she also teaches courses in botany, ecology, ethnobotany, and the ecology and restoration of plants of cultural significance to Native people. Her interests in restoration include not only restoration of ecological communities, but of our relationships to land. The mother of two daughters, Kimmerer lives in and gardens on an old farm in upstate New York.

Ursula K. Le Guin's study looks due north across the Willamette and Columbia rivers to Mount St. Helens, giving her a ringside seat at eruptions and a permanent excuse to stare out the window. She described her 1981 visit to the blast zone in a book of poems and prose, *In the Red Zone*. Born in Berkeley in 1929, Le Guin has lived for five decades in Portland. She has written many books of poetry and prose, in various modes—realistic fiction, science fiction, fantasy, young children's books, among others—all about more or less real places. Winner of numerous awards and honors, her most recent titles are a novel, *Voices,* and a volume of poetry, *Incredible Good Fortune.*

Poet and natural history writer **Tim McNulty** has explored the ancient forests around Mount St. Helens, planted trees on its slopes, climbed the pre-eruption summit in the 1970s, and has returned often since the 1980 eruption. McNulty is the author of six books of poetry, including *Through High Still Air,* and ten books of natural history, including *Washington's Mount Rainier National Park,* which won a National Outdoor Book Award. A revised edition of his *Olympic National Park: A Natural History* is due out in 2008. He lives with his family in the foothills of the Olympic Mountains.

Because **Kathleen Dean Moore** moved into her home in Corvallis, Oregon, on the day Mount St. Helens blew, all she retains of the top of the mountain is a glass bottle of ash scraped from the hood of her car. But mountaintops, rivers, and forests are the setting for her books of essays about our cultural and spiritual relations to wet, wild places—*Riverwalking, Holdfast, The Pine Island Paradox,* and her book in progress, *Wild Comfort.* Moore is Distinguished Professor of Philosophy, University Writer Laureate, and Director of the Spring Creek Project for Ideas, Nature, and the Written Word at Oregon State University.

Nalini Nadkarni has been called "the Queen of the Forest Canopy." A pioneer in forest canopy studies around the world, Nadkarni has conducted treetop research in Costa Rica and Washington State with grant support from the National Science Foundation and the National Geographic Society. A professor at The Evergreen State College, she received a Guggenheim Fellowship in 2001 to foster communication between scientists and nontraditional public audiences in churches, prisons, and legislative halls. She has organized "confluences" of ecologists, artists, poets, novelists, and dancers in remote field sites to share perceptions about nature.

Robert Michael Pyle, a life-long naturalist, has written *Wintergreen* (winner of the John Burroughs Medal), *The Thunder Tree, Chasing Monarchs, Walking the High Ridge, Sky Time in Gray's River,* and several acclaimed butterfly books. His book *Where Bigfoot Walks: Crossing the Dark Divide,* subject of a Guggenheim Fellowship, was inspired by experiences on the pre-eruptive Mount St. Helens. In recent summers he has studied blue butterflies that live on wild buckwheats adapted to the blast zone. Pyle is completing a novel and a collection of poems, and his column "The Tangled Bank" appears in each issue of *Orion Magazine.* He lives with artist and botanist Thea Linnaea Pyle along a tributary of the Lower Columbia River.

Born in Tennessee and reared in Ohio, **Scott Russell Sanders** studied in Rhode Island and Cambridge, England, and has taught for many years at Indiana University, where he is a Distinguished Professor of English. Among his more than twenty books are novels, collections of stories, and works of personal nonfiction, including *Staying Put*, *Hunting for Hope*, and *A Private History of Awe*. An early work, *In Limestone Country*, manifests his long-standing interest in things geological. Sanders' writing has won the Associated Writing Program Creative Nonfiction Award, the John Burroughs Essay Award, and the Lannan Literary Award. He and his wife, Ruth, a biochemist, have reared two children in their hometown of Bloomington in the hardwood hill country of Indiana's White River Valley.

A born-and-raised Oregonian, **Jim Sedell** has had a long, close relation with the mountains and waters of the Pacific Northwest. As an aquatic scientist at Oregon State University and the USDA Forest Service, he studied the streams of the Oregon Cascades and the lakes, hot springs, and streams of the area impacted by the 1980 eruption of Mount St. Helens. Sedell is Director of the Pacific Southwest Research Station of the Forest Service, which conducts natural resource science in California, Hawaii, and U.S.-affiliated western Pacific islands, and he has provided important leadership in the development of several major regional conservation strategies, such as the Northwest Forest Plan.

Gary Snyder's book *Danger on Peaks* is a testament to his life-long engagement with Mount St. Helens. A native of western Washington, Snyder spent several summers working as a fire lookout in the North Cascades and on trail crews, honing his engagement with mountain lands. Since 1970 he has lived in the watersheds of the South Yuba River in the foothills of the Sierra Nevada. The author of seventeen volumes of poetry and prose, including *Turtle Island*, *Axe Handles*, and most recently, *Back on the Fire*, Snyder has been the recipient of the Pulitzer Prize, the Bollingen Poetry Prize, and the Robert Kirsch Lifetime Achievement Award.

As a child, **Kim Stafford** spent a summer at a camp on the shore of Spirit Lake, a magic place turned to primordial soup by the volcano's blast in 1980. By the time he returned to the mountain in 2005, he was the founding director of the Northwest Writing Institute, and author of a dozen books, including *The Muses Among Us: Eloquent Listening and Other Pleasures of the Writer's Craft; A Thousand Friends of Rain;* and *Having Everything Right: Essays of Place*. Though older now, he remains in many ways that boy bent low to savor details on the mountain's ground.

Fred Swanson writes: "I have been a student, a connoisseur, and a lover of volcanoes since college days. Like a birder, I have a life list of encounters with erupting volcanoes—walking across an advancing *aa* lava flow at Arenal in Costa Rica, feeling the heat of fountaining lava on the flanks of Kilauea, sensing the deep seismic rumblings of Fernandina, Galapagos. But nothing beats my continuing affair with Mount St. Helens. What wonderful teachers. Hoping to share some of my interest in volcano science with others, I co-edited a book on the ecological responses to the 1980 eruption of Mount St. Helens (Dale et al. 2005, listed in Further Reading in this volume) and now this collection of impressions by creative writers and scientists."

A desert rat in a world of water, **Tony Vogt** lives and writes in the long shadow of Mount St. Helens, which looms figuratively over a bioregion that includes Corvallis, Oregon, where he teaches environmental philosophy and sociology. His research interests include the emergence of institutions for sustainability, such as watershed councils, co-managed fisheries, and programs that combine ecological restoration and ecological literacy. When Mount St. Helens erupted in 1980, he was with friends on top of Marys Peak, the tallest mountain of Oregon's Coast Range, and will never forget the ashen plume on the northern horizon, and the "May snow" that fell that morning.

Writer, artist, and naturalist **Ann Zwinger's** first book, about forty acres the family owns at 8,300 feet in the Rockies, was *Beyond the Aspen Grove* (1970), which she also illustrated. She wrote her second book, *Land Above the Trees,* with alpine ecologist Dr. Beatrice Willard. *Run, River, Run* won the John Burroughs Medal for Nature Writing, and in 1991 *Downcanyon* won a WESTAF Award. Her work appears in dozens of anthologies. She lives in Colorado Springs with her husband, Herman; they have three daughters, one of whom is also a natural history writer.

Susan Zwinger is an adventurer, naturalist, and writer whose explorations range from the eastern shrub-steppe lands of the Great Basin to the glacier-scoured volcanoes of the North Cascades. An illustrated journal keeper, she is the author of *The Last Wild Edge, Stalking the Ice Dragon, The Hanford Reach,* and *Still Wild, Always Wild,* a Sierra Club book celebrating the California deserts, and co-author of *Women In Wilderness.* She lives on Whidbey Island where she translates daily from Bald Eagle to English.

By Way of Thanks

When creative writers, philosophers, and other humanists get together with environmental scientists in an inspiring natural landscape to share ideas and insights, the results, in our experience, are so rich, unexpected, and provocative that it's hard to imagine how the separation of the disciplines ever occurred. This book is thoroughly interdisciplinary in its conception, in its methods, and, as you will see, in its vision. It was inspired by a field seminar, "Catastrophe and Renewal: the Mount St. Helens Foray," held in July 2005—four days of camping, hiking, and sharing insights on the mountain—sponsored by the Spring Creek Project for Ideas, Nature, and the Written Word and the Long-Term Ecological Reflections program. Many of the contributors to this volume participated in the Foray. The editors extend a deep bow of gratitude to those "Foraygers": John Calderazzo, Charlie Crisafulli, Jerry Franklin, Robin Kimmerer, Ursula LeGuin, Tim McNulty, Nalini Nadkarni, Robert Michael Pyle, Scott Russell Sanders, Jim Sedell, Kim Stafford, Tony Vogt, and Ann Zwinger.

Also with us on the Foray were several other important collaborators: our thanks to singer/songwriter Libby Roderick who gave to the Foray the extraordinary dimension of song; to Lynn Burditt, Deputy Forest Supervisor, Gifford Pinchot National Forest, for welcoming us to the Mount St. Helens National Volcanic Monument; to Nick Houtman, talented journalist with Oregon State University's Office of Advancement; to Mike Furniss (USDA Forest Service) for video, still, and audio documentation of the Foray; and to Oregon State University graduate students Jordan Baskerville and Michael Hanson who served graciously as camp-tenders and scribes. Gary Braasch, yet another integral part of the Foray, has been making stunning photographs of Mount St. Helens for three decades; we are deeply grateful for the use of his images for this book.

Others who provided invaluable help during the Foray: Maggie Dowd, Deputy Monument Manager, and Cheryl Mack, Archaeologist, both with the Gifford Pinchot National Forest; and Ray Chumley and family, backcountry caterers par excellence.

Funding for the Foray was provided by the USDA Forest Service Pacific Northwest and Pacific Southwest Research Stations. Two visionary scientists with the Forest Service have been steadfast supporters of Long-Term Ecological Reflections; we are grateful for the many contributions—fiscal, intellectual and creative—of John Laurence and Jim Sedell.

Thanks to Carly Johnson for inspired editing assistance, to cartographer Theresa Valentine for our maps, and to Mary Braun, Jo

Alexander, and Tom Booth at OSU Press for their many good services to the cause.

While we have tried to be as inclusive as possible in this collection, we hope it is only the beginning of the conversation about this magical area. We would like to see future conversations that include Native voices, those who work in the woods, civic leaders, and others.

Acknowledgments

John Calderazzo's poem "Mount St. Helens" was previously published in *ISLE*, volume 14.1, winter 2007.

Christine Colasurdo's contribution to this volume is an excerpt from her book *Return to Spirit Lake: Journey Through a Lost Landscape* (Sasquatch Books, 1997).

John Daniel's poem "To Mount St. Helens" was first published in his book *All Things Touched by Wind* (Salmon Run Press, 1994).

Tim McNulty's poem "The Way to Windy Ridge" was first published in *Origin*, 6th series #1, spring 2007.

Scott Russell Sanders' "Two Stones" © 2007 by Scott Russell Sanders, first appeared in *The Louisville Review* No. 62, fall 2007; reprinted by permission of the author.

"Pearly Everlasting" from /Danger on Peaks/ by Gary Snyder. Copyright 2004. Used by permission of the publisher.

Every effort has been made to contact Vijaya Mukhopadhyay, author of the poem, "Wanting to Move," quoted in Nalini Nadkarni's essay, or her publisher, to seek permission to use it in this translation from the Bengali and make proper acknowledgment, but this proved impossible by press time. The editors and publisher would be grateful for any contact information so that proper acknowledgment may be made in future editions of this book.